play with me

play with me

Living effusively with art

Sasa Hanten-Schmidt

Spector Books

**From now on
I’m going to live a joyful life
and enjoy my successes.**

Konrad Hanten-Schmidt

I'm just doing my job.

Ken

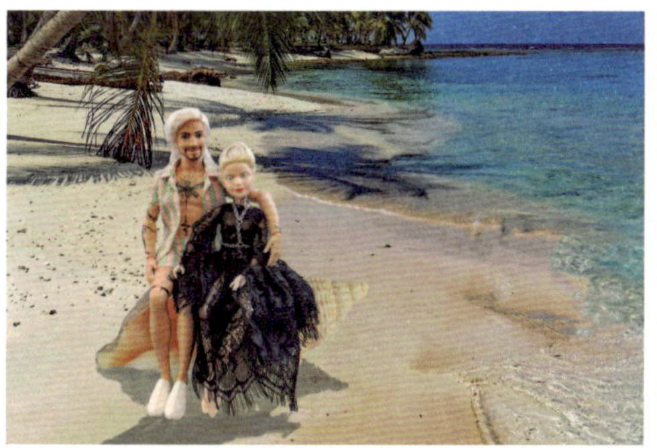

Markus Spatzier
BEACH

Gender designators are used arbitrarily. In cases of doubt, all genders are meant. If a particular gender only exists in one variant in reality, then it is designated as such; for example, art forgers tend to only be men.

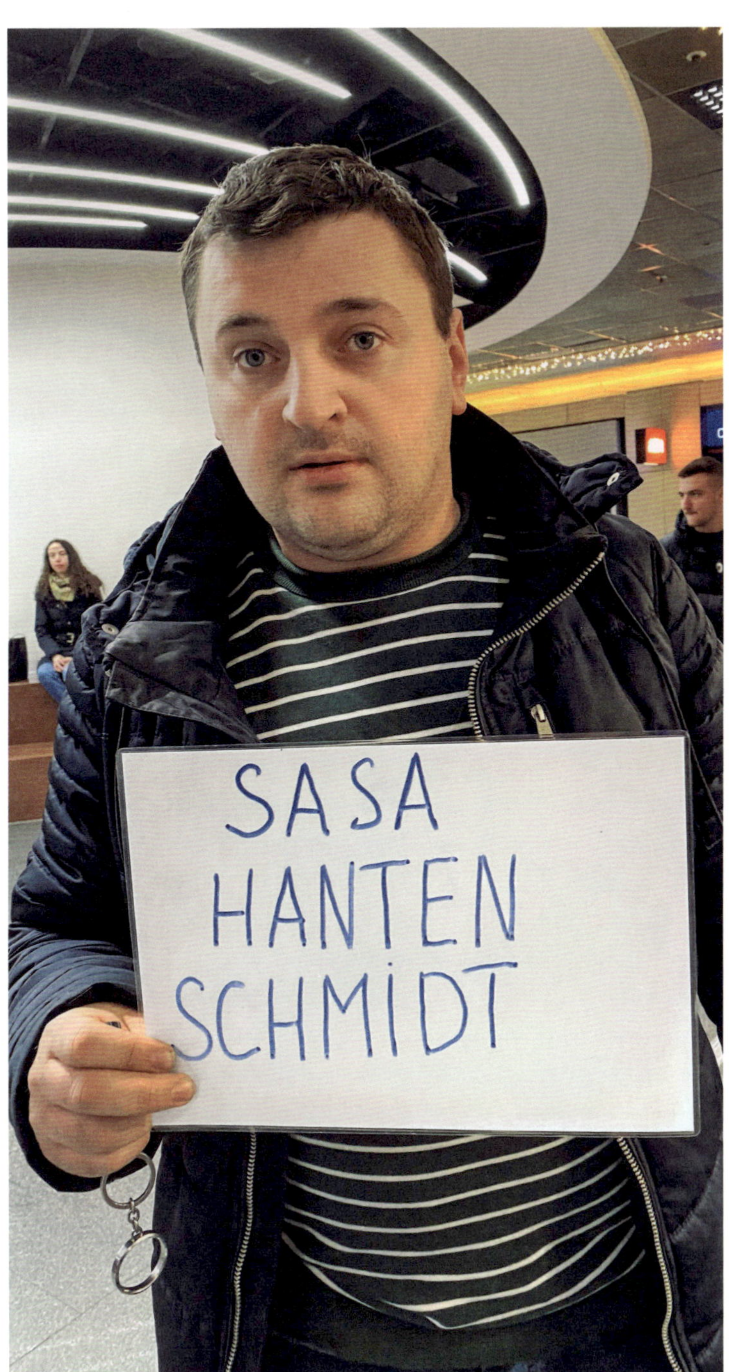

At the airport

London Heathrow. Out of the corner of my eye, I note that the plane hasn't yet arrived. Next to me, a woman asks a man wearing jeans and a jacket whether he thinks the flight will be on time. He thereupon starts deliberating whether an aircraft is available. Hang on! There isn't one in sight. Making a meal of it, he explains that yes, indeed we need to find that out first. Possibly we first have to wait for an aircraft to fly in. In our case, probably everything hinges on that. Slightly annoyed, I study the woman's face and scan it for any signs of a response to these extraordinary statements. None to be seen. The man continues, undeterred. Those flights that tend to usually be on time are those that originate here. He's nodding all the time. A case of personal-idiotic self-affirmation or simply of Tourette's. Well, I suppose I should beware of judging him. Or is he simply the reincarnation of a puppet on a stick from some Punch and Judy show? I decide in favor of version one as he proceeds, murmuring all the while in self-importance, to place everything in some far greater context: The key is, he suggests, always to fly in the morning, to get the very first flight out. What the…! It's 6.30 p.m. Still no sign of movement in the woman. And she remains frozen even when, conspiratorially and with a wink, he renews his worldly wisdoms. But then it is hardly worth paying for the hotel overnight, and the first flight out is invariably more expensive than any later ones. Now playing the real man of the world, he starts talking about the first flight as the "red-eye, as it were". Lurking to one side, I check through my fingertips to make certain there is no aircraft attached to the skywalk and wonder which of the two I find the crazier. I imagine turning to the woman and go through possible questions in my head, such as: "What can that man do that others can't?" I want to find out why this person, outwardly very attractive, ended up talking to such a guy. A guy who uses "red-eye" and "as it were" in a single sentence and can't see that there's simply no aircraft out there? From her gaze, I still can't discern an appropriate response forming. And what would I assume to be an appropriate response?

How about nausea, disgust? Maybe she's deaf and he hasn't realized. Is it only me who spots the empty jet bridge? So why is it I can see something he can't?

Seeing art – finding the mustard

Is the ability to spot something almost subconsciously out of the corner of your eye a skill acquired over decades spent studying art specifically at art fairs? No, or so I contradict myself immediately. After all, if it were the case that during any standard stroll round the art world, meaning with every air-kiss, as it were, you were noting things in the corner of your eye that you could later use to beneficial effect, then collectors would be able to apply the technique each time they scanned the fridge for certain things, such as the jar of mustard, and would obviously find it far faster than other mortals (meaning "men") with no links to the art market. My world is one that is simply teeming with men with immense experience of the art scene. Now none of them find, let alone cut, the mustard. Case closed. Hold on. Does my world include a control group of men with no links to Operating System Art? In my head I start parsing my contacts to basically heterosexual men, meaning those who never find anything, but likewise also have no links to the art market. I've got as far as "M" in my mental list of men before I find someone. Although I have no idea whether the golf pro in Vilamoura, Portugal, would find the mustard or not. Together with the skipper on Lake Geneva and the driver in Cologne, it's a pretty small control group I come up with. Well, my empirical social research fails when it comes up against the wall of the factual. The question will go unanswered. At which point I notice that in recent years I've grown accustomed to not letting men search for anything. Am I perhaps condescending? A fatalist? Or simply pragmatic? At any rate, it certainly means everyone gets on better and I easily achieve my 5,000 steps a day round the house without needing to even step outside. And all those steps are not the only benefit. It's always a game I play against myself. When I lay the table, am I focused enough and forget nothing? Can I foresee every possible eventuality related to the meal? Should I fail, I will have no alternative but to go and get what's missing myself, as I have absolutely no wish to once again hear those hated words uttered in my presence "Couldn't find it, it didn't move." And my meals with men are therefore a success. Avoidance strategies have fallen into disrepute for no good reason, if only because they are associated with avoiding what is actually right. Why not avoid everything that leaves you in a bad mood and can't be changed? In Vienna, a friend familiarized me with the term "Watschnbetteln" – begging for punishment. If you don't go around pleading to be smacked, you'll have a much greater time of things. All I can do is raise my sons to move through life differently. All those adults today who may be involved in spotting the contents of the fridge were raised by people whom I predominantly have never met. And in those cases where I have met them, I am abundantly aware of what must have gone wrong in the men's education.

To sell, you need to be humble

I find myself considering what I would actually get out of researching exactly what kind of erroneous socialization I face on each occasion. No point in brooding over it, information overkill isn't good for you. That's one lesson I've certainly learned at art fairs. Anyone wanting to sell something must avoid offering too great a selection and must not be too strategic. Buyers need to feel they've made a discovery and mustn't be disturbed in indulging their own chains of associations. Which is why most trade-fair booths are white. Each white cube objectifies things and likewise opens up a space for your own thoughts. In their heads, collectors can then imagine the picture hanging on the wall at home. The contents are something each person transposes into their own system of coordinates. How many years did I need to learn to not contradict thoughts on content and not to disturb when someone was busy making a positive decision to buy? Standing professionally on a trade-fair booth is a bit meditative at the end of the day. There's hardly any other occupation that is a more therapeutic purgatory than a job at a trade-fair booth, or so I believe. For ages nothing happens, and if it does, then you have to have patience in the decisive moment, albeit a special kind of patience. At times, hours may pass without anyone talking to you, although there are constantly people nearby, and then the person at the trade-fair booth is addressed and has to jump in as an active listener. It's especially hard to play the part of supportive listener if objective questions are being put to you. For example: "Is that a Penck?" while on the wall next to it stands written "A. R. Penck" in 40-cm-high adhesive letters, the artist has signed the work quite legibly, and next to the image there's a sticker on the wall declaring: "A. R. Penck, Self-Portrait, 1997". So answering the question is not exactly going to require knowledge, but rather superb sensitivity. And you need to make sure the spelling appeals to the age of the buyers, many of whom object, for example, to German's latest bout of new spelling. In my active days in the gallery business, the target group for high-priced items reacted to the new spelling the way a vegan reacts to a medium-rare entrecôte with no side orders. Incidentally, we sold the picture at the time only after we changed the title to "Untitled". Evidently, the title alone already made prospective buyers feel constrained in their choice. What exactly do visitors to such a fair want to hear, then? At the time, I had the same gut feeling as I did today at the airport. I start imagining dialogs that it would be best never actually come about, such as: "Someone was here yesterday and said his seven-year-old son Malte could have made it. Now we're selling the pictures by him, by Malte Schmitz. The stickers with the artist's name are left over from before. The price remains the same, 190,000 Euro. Really, it's truly just as good, and the paint's almost dried." Perhaps that's why I'm never bored. As only too often I catch myself dreaming up alternative dialogues. In the actual, real-life situation, I meanwhile function. That is the good-girl side to me. However, I do find myself a little embarrassed if I first reel off a few facts no better than Wikipedia, quote pretty accurately from essays on the artist, and then always elegantly manage to move things on to the absolutely imperative emotional realm. The seemingly personal reference always has to be created in a manner that will make the sale. Meaning I then add, as if as an afterthought, that we are so immeasurably proud to be able to put this museum-worthy piece on offer. Fresh for the market. After many years away from the eye in a major private collection. The idea is never to answer the original first question literally, but simply to lay the foundation and make a sufficient number of large pauses so that the collector, whenever she so wishes, can correct me, add things, or interrupt me. Because if they start thinking that I'm a bit silly or haven't really got any idea, then they'll also start thinking that the picture would definitely be better off with them at home. Magnificent! Then everyone's benefitting. Picture sold and they feel they were right. A win-win. Along the way, a few things can endanger success. Largely, the market players act in line with their roles, as if simply moving along set tracks. Out-of-place behavior during art transactions tends to be considered benevolently as socially-appropriate eccentricity. The only question that the seller will preferably answer with a committed voice, albeit without any commenting undertone, is that of the price. The fair setting, the location of the gallery at the fair, and the no-frills design of the trade-fair booth provide backup, and yet revealing what sort of a budget the buyer needs is the decisive moment in the interaction. The cognoscenti in the art trade sense what the prospective buyer now needs most: degradation, (pseudo-) intellectuality, or joviality. Something within this spectrum will stoke the fires of fear and greed and lead to the ink on a sales contract. The fear of being left out, and the greed to make a killing, to be ahead of the pack – those are the sources of energy driving high-end consumers.

Is buying art open to satire?

There are plenty of comedy sketches on art exhibitions, meaning on the rituals of private-view speeches and the like. By contrast, the world of luxury purchases has rarely come under the scrutiny of stand-ups or scriptwriters. We all know the jokes about the sales staff who, turning up their noses, make it abundantly clear they don't think you can afford the handbag. We've all experienced sales staff who find it helpful to say that they wear just the item themselves. How does one transpose these absolutely bizarre cases of authoritative role reversal into the world of the art market? One regular piece of self-importance: the sales staff simply ignore you. In the art market, everyone insists a deal gets sealed by a handshake, meaning it is quite usual for people to address each other informally. After all, both sides of the table rave about the same thing, and thus, as if they were discussing their favorite football club, words such as love and passion get repeated like some bloodless mantra. In order to whet the prospective customer's appetite and thus her wish to buy, like in schoolyards the wish to be part of the in-crowd is triggered. One tried-and-true method here is to suggest a monopoly on knowledge. Instead of announcing the price (see above) with a grand gesture, often the sales staff simply refuse to state the price in order to make it abundantly clear that you might want to be a customer but you're out of your depth this time. This behavior may be illegal, as there are clear regulations on prices being stated. However, the rules of the art market are different. There are numerous versions of this arrogant strategy of making it clear to someone interested in art that the market is one where you can feel fortunate to be offered a work but first have to prove that you are able to put the readies on the table. Gallery owners in Germany even have the audacity to name prices in dollars even though the fair is in the middle of Germany, or to make the person enquiring sweat in any number of different coded ways that you first need to hear, understand, and decipher. So, what exactly does 1 point 4 mean? What's their reference system? Who gets clobbered by this high-handed arrogance most and who gets off unscathed? Although there is a persistent rumor among collectors that the buyers with the deepest pockets at the fairs tend to be those who run around looking like homeless people, gallerists don't seem to take any heed of this particular urban myth. Old white men in cashmere pullovers are courteously welcomed. If white men show up with a female companion, only the men get addressed. So let me trash my idea of an art market cabaret. It is simply beyond satire. The way it is, all of this is anything but funny. How does one exaggerate any of this in a way that brings a smile to someone's face? Well, I for one don't have enough imagination for that. When I started out, I also could not have imagined that all this would actually persist down through the decades. In the art market, vapid and predictably conventional marketing strategies often contrast sharply with the object on sale. Intelligent, progressive, subversive art still gets sold in surroundings with Hessian wallpapering and alpha-male lookalikes. Unbelievable! For me, however, it is evidently possible to lead the right life in this false world because, despite ongoing marginalization and system-relevant objections, I have always liked working in the art business. The anachronistic market situation, the sheer effort of gathering together all the exhibits, carting them to a fair for only a couple of days, and then, under brutally dazzling light, trying to book the lion's share of the gallery's annual turnover – now that was a task that struck a chord with my personality. Most challenges in life are far less obvious. Well-trained patience and the ability to be keenly alert at a moment's notice when it comes down to it, and all of that without letting on that you've got to earn your supper super-quick – those are skills that are useful and which I always liked sharpening.

Andrei Roiter
N.Y. → 42

While still stuck waiting to board at Heathrow, I don't really think I'll need my patience. After all, here at the gate things will presumably unfold without the potentially energy-sapping delays. A quick glance around the cohort which has assembled on the seats in front of the counter for the flight leaves a positive impression. It consists mainly of individuals with sober, business-like hand luggage. I gauge that the setting speaks in favor of us all getting on board very quickly and the trip being quiet. Meaning the flight will be on time and tomorrow morning will start just as if I hadn't been away in the first place. I'll be in my own bed and will sleep well. That's worth its weight in gold. To quote the above well-versed babbler: Everything depends on that. Anyone who didn't go to boarding school and did not put down roots because they spent countless years in the traveling circus called the art market will possibly not realize how incredibly crucial this is. I really look forward to my own bed. And the fact that work and the kids mean we live in Cologne, Dresden, and Vienna has not prevented me from doing so. I've moored the selfsame bed in each of these three harbors. Which is something that has an additional benefit. The feeling that when I wake up in the morning, I first have to open my eyes to know which city I happen to be in – now that brings warmth to my heart. That act of waking up is like slipping into a pre-heated morning robe. Just like looking back on the time I spent in London. The trip likewise feels gorgeous and warm, as if I had lived each day exactly the way I wanted. That's what I call productive cognitive dissonance. Meaning what??? From the outside, things look completely unlike what I perceive them to be. Grandma Josefine would have said: "You're playing the Hegel and garbling things to sound right!" So what? As long as it works! If my working days are full to bursting, but I myself feel that one item in the diary follows quite naturally on from the one before with a light touch, then to my mind the project is successful. I go through the last few days in my head and think: That was great. Everything put in place, everything set in motion. No heavy lifting required. Everything explored and worked out in a pleasant atmosphere. To my mind, the team seemed motivated. Each of the members seemed grounded.

Konrad Klapheck, Claus Hugo Nielsen, Nan Hoover, Arnold Odermatt, Photo: Bettina Fürst-Fastré → 42

Even if, in the one or other case, this may not have been true. I've long since stopped troubling myself with inner reservations if everything functions on the outside. Business and depth psychology are not the best of friends. As with love. I think it's disastrous to dig too deep if everything is going well. It's all over the moment something is expressed, indeed sometimes the moment something is thought. Putting my finger on problems or playing "Find the Mistake" is something that is best left to the hours I spend compiling legal opinions. A girlfriend once told me she was busy delaying a date because she was a good two kilos too heavy in the event the two of them ended up in bed. Meaning she first wanted to lose the two kilos, or actually it was 2 ½. I often find myself pondering that sentence. Filing things away in the section for alternative dialogs, I would say: Never has a man said, on getting into bed with a new date, "no, first you need to lose 2 ½ kilos." For me, that is as good as unthinkable. Women and men live in two separate worlds, or so it seems to me. For women, it is somehow always about a couple of kilos less person. Either this is about physical weight per se, perceived to be too much, or all about the child thing: Yes, no, when, with whom…

Kabbalah-driven escapism

A few days ago, on one of my very rare walks, I read in the window of the "Chez Annette" boutique a card stating: "from 32 to 44". Between 32 and 44, that was great time in life, I thought. You've graduated, earned the one or other accolade, your bank account is far from empty, and in this core production period for academics the world is your oyster. The very moment that crossed my mind, I started to feel suspicious: Was I already entering dementia or had some other severe psychological abnormality befallen me? After all, or so I rationalized, what was written in the store window was not meant that way, and no one, but absolutely no one would

When the going gets serious all that helps is humor

share the way I saw it. However, if I break what I wrote down to the facts of the world surrounding me, then 32 to 44 is a range of clothes sizes, “Chez Annette” a bizarre, antiquated name for a couturier that has aged quite decently, and that phase in life between 32 and 44 is perceived by many women as a time in life where things are more than trying and you are enveloped in uncertainty. To be utterly blunt, I find my Kabbalah-driven escapism far better. Wherever at all possible, I ensure my propensity to daydream has its place in my life as a lawyer and court-appointed expert for art. Which is to say I have learned not to formulate any targets or otherwise appear businesslike. It’s far more effective to stay genuine, meaning in dream mode. And I was just successful precisely with that in London. In fact, there was enough space to present my great expectations for another shared future in such a charmingly mad way that no one could take offense. That, too, is an art with art: In each and every conversation the demands need to be put in a witty way, as I am not authorized to issue instructions to anyone. No, me, I have to motivate. Only then can a joke be grasped as a joke, and since it is out of court to demand that someone explain a joke, the demand does not leave any open flanks for attacks. For an exhibition held with works under commission, I therefore say: We don’t take anything back. Funny?

An artist cannot say to a gallery without causing some irritation that she wants everything in the show to go. In the best of all worlds, they’ll think she’s naïve; more probably, they’ll interpret such a statement as meaning everything has gone to her head. Conversely, galleries always want something new, fresh from the studio. Why? Artists are appreciated for their unique pictorial language. Logically, the exhibition should therefore be resplendent with typical, but new pieces. That is about as productive as saying to me just before the interview starts: "Be as excellent as always, but not too excellent, that'll make people aggressive." Not too excellent? So how does that work? That's like giving an alcoholic a cocktail and after he's taken the first sip saying: "There's only a splash of alcohol in it." I view demands for always-new things by people who afterwards only succeed, as always, in selling classics from the heart of the oeuvre as merely a mixture of power game and business ineptitude, neither of which bears commenting on further. I prefer to torpedo such discussions by myself, without there being any explicit substantive reason, banding sentences about that always include "I want". Unlike the artist, I don't find it difficult to formulate maximum demands. Because my role as head of the studio is unlike that of the artist herself. I am not representing here. I am not putting myself as a person on the line, as an artist is inseparably bound up with her works. An artist's agent is a third party. There's no general definition of how responsibilities are divided between the assistant and the impresario. To my mind, this lack of clarity and unpredictability is an asset. After all, it can also mean that you're good for at least one miracle. And my DNA straightforwardly lacks the harmony gene. I jest, but it's also true.

Diagnosis: No harmony gene

I am evidently less shy of conflicts and less in need of harmony than everyone else I know. I don't fear conflicts and instead prefer to bring things to a successful conclusion rather than try and superficially get by with someone in a given situation. Eschewing a conversation, avoiding clarifying things – both are not only socially inhibited but to my mind overly comfy, as in lazy, approaches. Anyone wanting to achieve a good result will need to critically engage with what others think and need. In that critical engagement, I find out what it is I do not like. That said, sometimes I also experience something such that I find myself being completely taken by a person. In heated debates, in a dispute where no holds are barred, sometimes everyone involved puts in a peak performance and finds out something new about themselves and the world. It is of course the case that in a debate it is often the differences that become especially tangible, and everything comes to a standstill. I'm happy to take that risk. Evidently, I am over-optimistic and very interested in people. Otherwise, I wouldn't often think that it's better to try and slug something out than to not try. After all, if necessary, you can simply halt mid-sentence and say, "Great, my blood pressure is now up and running. Let's get on with the agenda." Probably the greatest art of communication in life is to feel when it is worthwhile debating something and when any attempt to clarify things will simply trash everything. To resort to a dad joke to sum up what has been debated: Ask a man what he's thinking and it's all over. It's amazing how much lived wisdom is often to be found in such trivia.

Subversion – the weapon of the smart underprivileged

Since I traditionally have a lot to do and think, stacks of books await me, my bed awaits me (in other words, completely different but equally important stuff), I tend to avoid any unstructured encounters if they can instead be well arranged. Before the first people arrive and get to see the Angela Glajcar exhibition in London, in my capacity as head of studio I have long since left. In LOOK AT ME!

Checkpoints of an Art Collection (Spector Books 2018, together with Wolfgang Ullrich) I wrote that either I give a talk at the exhibition opening or I feel out of place there. This may sound arrogant, but it's part of a safety concept. At the lectern, the social pressure is less than it is in the audience, as my talk enables me to determine the topic that will be chatted about later. If I'm just standing around, then I have to be prepared for anything. Lately, I have developed a new, subversive strategy, namely to attend exhibition openings having taken a calculated risk: I hang from the wall. Because today artists use me as their model far more often than they did in the past.

Rosemarie Trockel
ANONYMOUS (section) → 42

Nowadays I am present and quite literally framed. Which is just as easy and is highly efficient in terms of the subplot of "working through that stack of books". Reading is like collecting art. One thing leads to another, the number increases rather than decreases, and the more you focus on something, the more you get the feeling that there's a mass of relevant stuff waiting to be discovered. What's great is to return full of curiosity and rejuvenated by fresh air to the stack of books. And that, too, is like collecting art. Because if you return tired, not to say exhausted, to your own art collection, then all you'll see are the gaps, and you won't forgive yourself for the things you bought that you should have ignored.... In this regard, my brief absence this time from my desk and the places where I can sit down and study has gone ideally well, as it was completely free of any aggression. In other words, occasional dates where I have to be physically present are still OK – and indeed on occasion really helpful, I say to myself, inwardly satisfied. Which is why, in this instance, I don't deduct any points for having to leave the house. An insistence on physical presence in the sense of constant "meetings" is something I simply find irritating. But in this case, it was all good. No opportunity for slipping into one of the dark side-streets of life, into some trance that revolves around problems, around bemoaning how awful everything is. In such instances I'd rather play the idiot and sit grinning, as if long since a borderline moron. I can't get over the fact of just how good everything was. Incidentally, I even found time to buy my Christmas presents. In September. Not that this is unusual for me, and rather a hangover from my conventional years in boarding school. The weeks before Christmas are supposed to be a time of contemplation, not of hustle and hassle. And I accordingly make certain that by the end of November everything's done and those four weeks before Christmas are dipped in candlelight and there are no cares in the world. The nuns' superciliousness toward secular teachers and mothers who spent the run-up to Christmas without time to even fix their hair impressed me deeply. We harmless convent students were regularly sent to confession; I took the nuns' arrogance fully onboard, and it provided me with the material for my own, pretentious confessions. Because I found it a bit mad to confess. Perhaps it was simply a cultural technique that bore rehearsing for a rainy day, I asked myself. Conversely, that would mean that a wild and sinful life must await each and every one of us pupils. So I really looked forward to that wild life and bridged the time spent waiting by properly rehearsing the cultural technique of the "confession". I didn't bother dreaming things up for it like the others, who for example claimed to have smacked their younger brothers. Which was in itself a complete lie and therefore in turn the stuff of a confession. I preferred to put the priest through his paces with complicated statements such as that I liked the nuns' superciliousness. He had a tough time with me cognitively. Which I also liked, and thus I had already provided a reason for a few more Ave Marias, namely arrogance. While my fellow students feared the date in the booth, I really looked forward to these sophist performances. An intellectual Pippi Longstocking, as it were. Is the propensity for subversion something acquired? Is it a reflection of power structures that you cannot overcome? Possibly a survival tactic for the over-clever underprivileged? I made my peace with it and enjoyed giggling away inside. Meaning that I am utterly balanced this very moment. Well, up to this moment, that is.

Andrei Roiter
REFUGE → 42

Elves don't wear wristwatches

"Have you taken a pregnancy test?" – the sound of an unmodulated female voice interrupts the tranquility at the airport gate. "Of course, I did a pregnancy test. Four weeks ago, at home, back in Berlin. Negative," comes the jarring answer; it feels like the person is directly behind my head. "What?", declaimed such that not only everyone on the padded seats can really hear it, but everyone else and said in a strident, truly alarmed manner: "C'mon? Pregnancy test four weeks ago?! So, you could in fact be pregnant." With lightning speed, I survey the faces in the row sitting opposite me. Are they also doing the math? Yes, they are. My eyes tell me that a whole series of other passengers has likewise already reached a conclusion. One man rolls his eyes, another is smiling to himself mischievously and raising an eyebrow. A woman exhales indignantly and looks at her watch. How cool is that? The woman has a wristwatch, I bow down before such luxury. I last owned a wristwatch at the age of nine. It has a Snoopy watch face. Why does anyone need a watch, the child in me giggles to itself. A wristwatch is a prime feature of distinction, my inner super-smart child retorts. Well, I could differentiate more here: My attitude towards the object of use in question possibly stems from a conventional upbringing. At boarding school, the day had a clear structure throughout, and a watch was completely superfluous. I later found that anyone who needs to check the precise minute of the day seems to be dependent on things, lacking in freedom, whereas someone who does not know roughly what time it is, meaning the hour, doesn't suitably relate to the world around them. Today I find wristwatches a meaningful mark of social distinction. There was a time when you could tell from the kind of bows on shoes whether someone cared for themselves; today there are so many ways to get round tying your shoes correctly that having a wristwatch is a true blessing. I am now reconciled to watches the way I realize a horse can be my friend, or a particular food. I don't wear a watch, not in order to make a statement nor because I am too poor to do so, but simply because I refuse to play along. As regards those who do play along: Yes, I try to read the mark of distinction correctly. Omega or Rolex? Longines or Swatch? Or, like the clearly ironic-self-confident lady opposite: a men's wristwatch, old, and of course an automatic. A. Lange & Söhne. Cap duly doffed!

In general, this auditorium seems not to have wanted the conversation but now wants definitive answers as to what happens next. No one rustles a newspaper. No one looks at a phone screen. Everyone waits. And I doubt anyone expected the irritated answer that comes boomeranging: "I still don't believe you!". All eyes that I can see are suddenly wide open. Fertility as a matter of belief? Damnation! I shall blunt my disadvantage of having my back to the scene. Now I really want to know who is coming out with such stuff. And I don't disguise my curiosity. Sure, I could easily do so, pretend to be looking for someone. Instead, I adopt a pleasant, open demeanor and turn round, expectantly. And am promptly dissatisfied. How stupid of me. What on earth was I thinking? Capricious Amazons in elegant silk dresses? Faced with the facts, I am inwardly up in arms: No way this plot would make it into a script. Too much stereotyping, the producer would say. And misogynous into the bargain. Filling female roles with toneless, squeaky high voices is derogatory in the extreme. However, in this case reality is not politically correct, and again the setting does not lend itself to satire. This cabaret is as dead as a frozen fishfinger. How to describe, how to point up this picture? Impossible. Two no longer really young women, say in their early 30s, leisurely coiffured, leisurely clothed, and with stubborn faces, sprawled on backpacks. Around them, shapeless bags and pouches of different sizes stuffed full. Drinks containers stick visibly from the outside pockets of the backpacks or stand open on the floor. The environment looks as if it would not smell particularly nice. At the same time, everything somehow seems like it was washed in the deep past using bleach and dried flat, under a dog. This clothing has never come into contact with proper laundry, let alone a clothes hanger. And this is definitely beyond the pale of color blocking, let alone radiance. The setting is completely beyond belief. Surrealism would immediately set in if one of the two "Berliners" were now to speak with a southern accent. Then the caricature would be perfect. I am a little confused that all of this is happening live. Perhaps I should look around and see where the camera team is hiding. It is too impossible to be true: How can these Germans think that in an international airport, in the waiting area at the jetway for a flight to Vienna, people won't understand them? Ladies, in case you forgot, in Austria, German is the official language! Irrespective of how little we may understand of how German is used locally. The overarching idea is that – it's German. Like a lot of things in Austria, the relationship to the German language is likewise a one-way street. Which is to say that they understand everything we say. And, conversely, we hear what words are spoken but do not understand the meaning. Nonetheless. Here at the gate for the Austrian Airlines flight, almost without exception everyone understands what the conversation is all about. Hard to imagine that the two with their hands constantly in their hair or in their "beetroot chip" bags don't notice this. It was a long path I took in life until I grasped that in situations which I deemed should be damned, it bore consideration that there might be an acceptable explanation, i.e., in the referential system used by those I condemned.

Socially adjusted alternative behavior

The question is whether the two could have discussed the whole thing differently or could even have behaved differently – from the worm's eye view. After all, pregnancy is at times an explosive topic and perhaps really does need to be talked over. That much I can accept. To my mind, the socially adjusted behavior seemed obvious. Even small changes in the spoken text would have made the conversation less intimate: test instead of pregnancy test, and in the post-Corona-world no one would have had reason to prick up their ears or raise an eyebrow. Is it not rather the case that the two wanted to be heard and understood? What image of themselves did they therefore want to convey? Somewhere between Babylon Berlin and a giveaway drugstore brochure? Welcome to TV for the lower classes! No, I don't at all like the associations I had. I don't want to think any of this. I want to be back in my study-cum-store, which I tenderly call my comptoir. My comptoir, that's where I can sit and write, my refuge. My study-store is a symbol of not having to leave the house in order to achieve something, experience something else, or get to know someone. Everyone comes to my place. That's gone just fine for ages now. For weeks I only walked the 60 meters between my apartment and the store. The lockdowns during the pandemic hardly impacted my life negatively. Fewer people walked by my store window, yes. But conversations could at times be held outside – depending on the weather, all wrapped up in a blanket on comfy seats, and the beverages changed depending on the time of day or topic (coffee/sparkling wine). How quickly rituals then evolved: I put the blankets in the laundry basket in the early evening and carried the chairs back inside. Everything had to be washed and disinfected. Days ended early. That was absolutely fine by me.

Life goals: not open to blackmail and no bad conscience

When I was a junior lawyer, one of the court trainers said to me, really just in passing, that she had given up smoking to avoid being open to blackmail. She now no longer had to sum things up quickly only because her body was insisting it was time to go outside for a smoke. Since she knew the pattern owing to her own past as a chain smoker, she now conversely made careful use of the prospect of a cigarette break in order to influence the parties involved and to bring proceedings to a conclusion. In other words, she confided in me, you need to check your own idiosyncrasies to establish what can be used in your favor. Nothing is only good or only bad. Did I get her drift? And she promptly answered her own question: “Probably none of this means much to you. You’re very young still and comparatively inexperienced.” Indefinite legal concepts such as age, experience in life, casually thrown into conversations by our trainers. Now that was a reason not to like the course I was on. Why couldn’t these people simply behave? Why was the judge wearing shorts and a short-sleeve checked shirt when I was sworn into the bar, exposing his chest, or rather, his breasts, in the process? They were larger than mine. I had dressed with appropriate aplomb for the occasion and wanted to take this next step in my career with grace. Today, I would put it to him in a resounding rhythm: “This is the end. My only friend. The end.” And send him crashing in flames. Over. How to preserve one’s composure? How to make something out of the situation? For people like me, menus with little pictures are ideal. That way, the horizon of my expectations is carefully set, like the table hopefully. Without such support, I sometimes catch myself stepping into a trap of my own making, that of imagining how I would have done it rather than how the person actually in charge of things should have done it. Meaning that I am a Romantic. That's an advantage in my private life, I feel, but it gets in the way here. Being sworn in as a fully qualified lawyer is something I imagine happening in an auditorium. The judge in full robes, a normal court day, meaning other business going on, the buzz of people coming in and out, the judge asking everyone to stand, and I then speak the words after him. Then he wishes me good luck and says something edifying and encouraging, some lawyer proverb such as: "See you in court, Madam Colleague." Sadly, it's not to be. Or, as the lawyers would say: minus. Instead of any of that, we're in a dingy office with a few potted succulents on their way out of life and he pushes a (well) thumbed sheet of paper over the desk with the oath written on, which I'm now supposed to read out. He then stands. I get my bearings: My oath is to be made on the constitution of the State of Hessen, or "Heesen" as the piece of paper would have it. Heesen not Hessen – such bad spelling and the constitutional state seem to be as closely wed as is my wish to become a member of the legal profession with my urgent need to blow the whole place up. But I'm fighting for my happiness. After all, I spent years working toward this one day, studying for it, I even ate in the canteen twice during all those years (for personal reasons). Instead of beginning, like a governess I inform the judge "Mr. Chairman, I wish to give my oath without swearing by a religion. I do not wish to involve Jesus in the matter." My timing is perfect, raising my eyes during the last sentence from his sandals to his breasts. Now he's inhibited. I take note of the feeling. Saying something surprising, essentially evidencing a good upbringing – that is at the same time almost being lascivious, now I needed to perfect that. With the ex-smoker, I had been pretty close to the concept. For her, I had outlined things in a legal examination format like recitals: My ancestors were all farmers. For centuries. Farmers go out when there's something to be done. Sow the fields, bring in the harvest. Farmers do most of their work in the farmyard or within their own four walls. It is to this that I attribute my propensity only to leave the house if something important needs to be done that requires my presence. People who come from families in which everyone leaves the house, on the one hand to work and, on the other, for every potato, call me a desk-potato. Legally speaking, one could well say that I am not sensitive to being locked up. Their astonishment was almost as profound as the shock in the corridors outside court if someone were to say "enjoy lunch" to me and I were to gaily reply "and may yours be awful". Little sensitivity to being locked up sounded back then like a useless ability. The pandemic taught me different. Back then, at least, it was pretty clear that some employed position outside the house was not very suitable for me. Specifically in law offices, a strict regime of continual presence prevails. That seemed crazy to me. If the field has been harvested, then you go home. If you harvest swiftly, then you go home earlier. Work with no natural end sounds not only like something imposed from outside but also like a lack of successes. Since a dearth of new young lawyers has set in, the mindset has clearly started to change as regards always being physically present in the office. Although maybe that's just a big-city myth. At any rate, the part about there being fewer young lawyers is certainly true. The Baby Boomers are busy retiring and the smaller cohorts that follow are increasingly steering clear of the tough law courses with the risky major exams at the very end. Over half the students are female. In some places times do not change after all. The extensive law courses are followed for many women by uneven professional biographies. Interruptions, part-time employment. I would be astonished if anybody in the larger law offices ever thought about things like reconciling family and professional life when it came to hiring mercenaries.

Amazing how much you can pack into a single life. I feel like a monarch who sees an entire football team (and some of the members on the bench) overtake me as heads of state. When I was a young lawyer, I tended to greet colleagues with whom I had arranged to meet for supper at 7 p.m. with the words: “How truly endearing: You’ve taken half a day off for me!” Had I been admitted to the bar today, it would perhaps have been less imperative for me to seek a career in an exotic field such as art. Today I would possibly fit in elsewhere, too. Questions that are long since by the by. Thankfully, everything has gone well with my choice of specialist work. “Only” art. However, the human factor on the other side of the table of course remains a strain. Not only during the actual work, but also along the paths that I sometimes have to tread. As with the grand moment when I was sworn in, I had dressed appropriately well for my flight; after all, a dress is both armor and a battle robe, and I had imagined that with my duly sized, albeit eccentric, hand luggage I would be able to travel without hitches. In flight, I would drink a glass of good Austrian beer and take a photo of it which, on landing and while waiting at the baggage claim belt, I could then send to my female friend who brews it. To be honest, I had already polished up a caption to accompany it. “It was written in the sky: Beer is the proof that God loves us.”

In Germany I don’t feel ashamed o other Germans (unless they are relatives)

Instead, here were my thoughts being scattered by the two women with their backpacks. I do not like people who make me think that I am a bad person, and I really disliked the two chip-eaters as a consequence. I suddenly worried that because of them I might not be in bed in time to get up refreshed the following morning. Boarding with all that nonsense? In Germany, I don't feel ashamed of other Germans (unless they are my relatives). In England, I can feel ashamed of all other Germans or people who are thought to be Germans. In this context, I feel myself to be a European. Now is England part of Europe or not? I admonished myself to stop tormenting myself, although I did, at the same time, dearly hope that my business-class ticket would pay off, and I would not have to sit in the immediate proximity of the woman who was potentially pregnant and did not want to be and her companion. My reserves of feeling shame for others had already been exhausted before the situation at the airport. Because the prior evening there had been a German artist among the guests at the dinner table. Not the artist I represent. And since I do not really hold her work in high regard, I was a little concerned that I would possibly have to try and wriggle my way around having to offer an opinion on her oeuvre. It is far more gratifying in life to be introduced to people you revere. Although there is possibly then a greater risk of having one of those evenings where the best quips all occur to you in the taxi on the way back to the hotel. Because I want people whom I admire to like me, and I seek to be a leisurely and entertaining neighbor at table. At that moment, all of this played no role. I was sitting with my group in the customary setting. Talk was fun, and a bit over the top at times. We were very much able to enjoy the great restaurant and the attentive staff as if we were back on a school trip together. The artist in question, however, took no notice of us whatsoever. She conversed exclusively with a collector whom the host had placed next to her. The host owns a gallery that represents the artist, among others. The gallerist was evidently sparing himself the labor and left it to the artist herself to talk about her work and even to mention that she was not yet included in the gentleman's collection. At our end of the table, we were more or less unanimously of the opinion that we should feel sorry for the collector, as she really was nailing him down. On the other hand, we had no real sense of needing to rescue him, as, or so we agreed, he was an adult after all and able to defend himself. There was also more or less unanimity that the artist was overshooting the general need in the market to talk about oneself by urging the man directly to buy.

Division of labor in the art market

A ghastly error in the field of the social division of labor. Artists produce art. Gallerists sell it. Museum guys and gals exhibit it. Art historians compile catalogue raisonnés. A clear structure of who does what. So much for the theory. How often do museum people actually broker sales? How many catalogue raisonnés are produced in galleries and (surprise, surprise!) editions by rivals not contained in the lists? How often are the works in a museum exhibition up for sale? Recently, I stood in a great museum show and was enthusing about it when the gallerist said to me, “Hang on a mo’, I’ll get you the price list. All the pieces on show are ours.” Just as strange: With a voice as monotonous as a robot, at the preview and opening events for all the lenders the curator of the retrospective outlined the artist’s biography, starting with his place of birth, through what primary school he went to, and on to where he studied. At long last, she named a few important work groups. There was no one in the hall who did not already own a couple of these important works. As a lender, you assume you may have to forgo having your artwork within your own four walls for a few years as exhibitions increasingly hang forever in museums and then even go on tour, because you are serving general research on the oeuvre. Anyone who by this point has had no doubts as to the meaningfulness of loaning out a work now knows they are wrong. Since the unjoyful person, who stands so close to the microphone to speak that it’s almost certainly already moist, goes even further and explains with the constrained range of her emotional timbre that the artist selected the works himself and expresses her gratitude with no change in tone that he also handled the hanging. Cheers to scholarly reflection! Let no one say that women who have managed to make it into a museum position are not diligent and conscientious, and all of them perfectionists who are therefore hard to work with. Oh no, lassitude and blunders are not gender specific. From there, it is a small step to certification on the back of photos to guarantee their authenticity and to bagging higher six-digit sums for these "expert" opinions. For lassitude and greed really go well together. All the overlaps in professional reach lead at some point or other to complications. Or so practice shows. In the ideal world of this dinner, however, we're a little tough on the man who's paying for our meal. The gallerist should really do his own job. On the other hand, in line with my training I immediately take his side (think: the question as to the correct alternative, worm's-eye perspective, etc.) and claim that maybe from his point of view he's

done everything right. Perhaps he simply wanted to give the collector an opportunity to get to know the artist. That's a perfectly good motive, surely. And maybe he intended to build on it afterwards? Or did he simply sacrifice the collector? Maybe he wanted to burden the collector with the artist so that the rest of us could have a great evening undisturbed by her? Whatever angle you took, each seemed justified, and until we got round to ordering dessert everything was going smoothly. While almost everyone else at table was well-manneredly taking receipt of the menu again and studying the list of delicacies, the artist announced she was intimately familiar with the place, in fact had as good as been born here, so, no, she didn't need the menu. And, anyway, it didn't matter where you went in London, the desserts were always the same.

Everyone understands German you just have to speak loudly

For the first time that evening, I felt something bubbling up in me which my hairdresser calls my "finickity-ness". After all, I always tell my children that we are guests, and one should never pass generalizing judgment on the cuisine of another country. Furthermore, I always tend to say, you can cook anything well – or not. Even pumpkin soup is potentially edible. "It's just the same" is objectively and linguistically not true. While, inside me, I was still running the routine review of the artist's behavior, the situation was already escalating. She informed all and sundry that since we were taking our time she would simply go ahead and order her cheese. Turning to the waiter she continued: "Yes, Mancheddar on the cheese plate." Turning to the person sitting next to me, I smirked: "Superb Hitler English. Stunning this woman." The waiter simply waited. Good man. She insisted: "Mancheddar. And bread." When this did not prove successful, she promptly upped the decibels, and people at other tables started to turn their heads. So it was that she ended up with a high-pitched: "I want Mancheddar cheese." Everyone was trying to stare at their feet, helpless to obviate things. I heard myself say to nobody in particular: "Did you know, incidentally, that people understand German all over the world? You just have to speak loudly and clearly enough." To this day, I do not know whether what the artist wanted was Manchego or Cheddar. I persuaded her to simply order the specialty of the day, a sorbet variation. Matter closed. Once a mere anecdote in history, things can be really funny. They can, however, be deeply problematic when experienced first-hand with no escape route. And this is specifically the case for those things that occur in life that have the desired potential to be anecdotes, but where suffering the real situation gets tortuously protracted and ever-new details don't make something any funnier. Things should fade away into the realm of the anecdotal as soon as the main joke has been said. Exactly that was the case with my flight home. Because that evening, up in the skies with Austrian Airlines, I was to experience an almost intolerable amount of insufferable commentary as material filling time. Before the trolley made its way down the aisle with my beer, I was already fully acquainted with the details of the potential father of the child – Benny, 33, from Stuttgart, now a resident of Moabit, Berlin, uni dropout and occasional DJ. The two were back very much within hearing range. Another heavy dent to my prejudices. Why were these two faux hippies flying business? Not that Benny had any prospect of getting my sympathy. After all, the guy had decided to bag a woman who wore leggings instead of pants. There are objects that people who, to my mind, are my equals and with whom I would therefore duel simply do not possess. I understand the notion of fashion that strides down a catwalk in an army camo-look; I get the concept of tracksuits as festive garb; but the individual parts will always be discernible as what they are. Bodies clad in catwalk-ready tight tracksuit bottoms are different. No matter if they are a 32 or a 44. Sure, Lagerfeld's claim that anyone who owned jogging pants has lost control over their life may be partly out of date, but in this case, it's spot on. Leggings! I didn't need to know more about Benny than what I saw. The pronouncement that he was a real loser who screwed but had a screw loose was perhaps a tad unfair and attributable to the emergency hormonal state of the speaker who was in the early weeks of pregnancy. Substantively it was no doubt true. While I was enjoying my beer nonetheless (attributable first to the fine beer and second to my level of frustration), I spied the advantage. Otherwise, I would also be faffing about with some other preoccupation and making things complicated, for example reading a newspaper while handling the beer, which means a bottle and a glass, which together means three items and two hands. In this instance, there was no way I could read. On the other hand, reading the newspaper I always find out something new. Or something confusing. For instance, I read a review of an exhibition by Rosemarie Trockel. I am well-acquainted with the oeuvre, the artist is well represented in my own collection, and on occasion she hires me as a model.

Rosemarie Trockel
SASA → 43

I had prepared myself for the exhibition in question; the talk the director gave at the opening seemed logical to me, albeit not inspiring, but sound, journeyman stuff. The review of the exhibition seemed to come from a parallel universe. Now I am a slow reader. At times, people object: “How can someone who is as talented as you read so slowly?” I’ve grown accustomed to answering: “Because I want to remember it afterwards. Forever.” I read the review in question twice, slowly. It gave an erroneous account of the curatorial concept, and highlights of the exhibition were presented absurdly. Gosh, I thought. If something is printed in the paper that is completely and utterly wrong about something that I can judge, how often do I then read something that is wrong and do not know because I cannot judge it? The conversation about Benny provided no new details. Meaning no fact. As in the interpretation of a poem, the focus was exclusively on elaborating on feelings and airing assumptions. I don’t even know what Benny would have answered to the question of what would change by having a child, whether he would then no longer go back to his parents for Christmas. I think that if you no longer need to go back to your parents at Christmas because you have your own child, then I would have been pregnant as a sophomore. Without that additional benefit, things dragged on. 35. Just another case in point that the right incentives weren’t there! In the course of the conversation, my view of the admonishing friend starts to change. Incidentally, it turns out she’s called Corinna. Initially, she expressed concern that her friend might be pregnant by "that guy". So far, so understandable. And now she's quacking on about the biological clock ticking and that you shouldn't wait too long to have children. So, what's it going to be Corinna? Hand on heart, Corinna, are you bitchy and frustrated, or calculating, or whatever? Do you think there is a correct alternative option? To this day, I am uncertain how the matter at hand should be judged. Reproduction planning is always tough. An equation with a lot of unknown variables. If we wish our acquaintance had long since got pregnant, then we can discuss the weather and not the "whether". Seen this way, a child can be considered an advantage. To what extent Benny was (going to be) involved, now that is another story entirely. What I found interesting about the talk the two were having was that onboard it was clear that everything was open, and nothing could be decided for certain. Which has a literary quality to it. The inflight shopping magazine didn't offer pregnancy tests. There was no talking with Benny. I mean, there wasn't even WLAN as a fallback. The facts of the matter were completely uncertain, the issues existential and complex, and at this stage it was all only speculation rather than definitive statement. And what exactly did "only" mean here, I wondered. In this interim stage, conversely everything is possible. Is it not a primordial human condition, the wish to imagine? To dream?

Ready to play?

Letting your thoughts wander and indulging in a bit of daydreaming is a good way to prepare yourself to sleep deeply. While asleep, we all tend to work through the previous day, so I try to work through the day while it's still day. When I wake up, I don't have time to jot down my dreams; no, I want to get on with experiencing the day. Meaning after the very first cup of coffee. That said, I take daydreams seriously and note them down – the feeling of walking past an empty house or a closed shop and imagining: What would I turn that into? I've known that feeling since childhood. Isn't that something we all share? A castle, a farmyard, an empty shop window. Doesn't that set things in motion? Don't we all start buzzing with what-if fantasies? Or do such thoughts reveal me to possess the mind of a collector and therefore all the not-so-nice attributes of needing to be admired, to be able to influence things? Am I somehow similar to the clients I support (and they include the collectors, after all)? Although all I do is write expert valuation opinions, I like to resort to the word "support" because it sounds so helpless – on their part. That's my little aggressive poke at those who think none of what I do is particular important; it's quickly done, an irritating but necessary step along the way to ownership. Essentially, the expert opinion should be on the table a few hours after the client commissions it and should reflect the result they want to see. And I should, of course, wait a few weeks before sending them the invoice.

Power games with unpaid invoices

Collecting has something to do with a game. Game theorists have all sorts of difficulties working things out. Probably this is why there's so much haggling. It's not about money. It's all about the game. About the thrill, the feeling of power. This is wide terrain: who it is the invoice goes to, how much it is for, whether it is then left collecting dust on a desk and the collector waits until he gets sent a payment reminder, and how, if at all, he responds to such reminders (on a spectrum between "outrageous" and "how tactless, we're friends are we not?"). If you don't play the game, you're a spoilsport. All that helps is a joke. If you hire me, it's now like dry-cleaning: Pay in advance. Or: Time is money. No discounts unless the cash hits the account within ten working days. That means: The bank confirms it's dropped. Not: Yes, I've credited it to your account. Why the exact ten days? Because it sounds so official. A round number, not 9 ¾ as in Harry Potter and not 10 ½ like the chapters in Barnes' History of the World. Most recently, I issued an invoice to a bank. I had been expected to pen the opinion quickly. The client needed to report its assets and liabilities, and time was getting short. Tax filings and balance sheets are like Christmas: They always occur suddenly and unexpectedly, and someone somewhere is pressed for time. So, I hit the gas pedal and delivered. When I sent a reminder that the payment of my invoice was outstanding, I was informed that it had to be countersigned by a member of the board, which was why it was taking so long. To which I (promptly) replied: "I thought you were a bank, and now it is you who wants me to give you a loan." In the gallery, I soon learned that to be a happy person you need to put a price tag on waiting times. My mentors termed this an "act of emotional hygiene". Worried waiting and frustrated uncertainty are the inescapable attributes of romantic relationships. And they are appropriate there and without exception have the desired function: You take a good look at yourself, learn something about yourself, about the other person, and can take the opportunity to be humble and to wallow in the sweet pain of yearning. So far, so good. But in business life, worried waiting for the inflow of funds is poison for your self-confidence and your business. Meaning: Never trust someone in advance, but expect payment in advance. In the case of current business relationships, the rule must be: Anyone who delays pays. Or anyone who keeps the art for far too long "on approval" or has purportedly mislaid the invoice or never received it pays more next time.

Abating waiting

The at times tense wait until invoices are paid is another test of patience (not only) in the gallery business. An exercise in humility. Meaning here we have a real dilemma. Having to wait is a kind of uncertainty, and uncertainty makes you nervous. And yet nervous is exactly what you should not be. You need to try and seem cool and in charge of the situation. Small wonder that this system means the players are constantly tense, and that this in turn spawns very strange character traits. For all my admiration for the gallerists who have lined the path of my career, I sometimes think: If I were you, then I would rather be me.

What consequences does this have for my life? If I'm asked why I married "this" collector and not another man, then sometimes I simply put it this way: He only buys in galleries and does not sidestep the trade, and what is more he pays his bills, immediately. Kids have a name for that: scout's honor. In the general discourse among collectors, the focus tends to be on different things. Attempts to distort the competition with studio purchases and haggling as if in a bazaar are not of interest. It is more like everyone wants to claim presumptuously that their own collection of art is of great interest to the general public, that as businesspeople they have a clear idea of how to establish a museum and are in fact better able to do so than "the public sector"; that's the kind of thing you'll hear. The private museum is well-suited for a collective thought experiment among the collectors.

Exhibitionism – the private museum

A museum of your own is considered the absolute pinnacle of private collecting activities. The private exhibition space – that is purportedly what all collectors dream of having. Which makes me ask: Then why don't they all do it? Compared to the prices paid on the art market, for the price of a single new piece you could easily afford to rent exhibition spaces of your own for quite a while. There's no need to immediately go about building your own halls. So let me rephrase: Is it only outstanding collectors who discern, in every abandoned butcher's shop and every shop window where a few forlorn, yellowing, thick support stockings hang, an opportunity to design something, to infuse the space with new life? Is it not normal to more or less give oneself over to daydreams and, incidentally, to leave it at that? Because of course such thoughts likewise occur to me, I have never before asked anyone. I mean, whom should I ask? I can't even find a control group for the question of the unsuccessful search for unpopular items in a fridge. Empirical social research is simply rendered difficult by the fact that you live in a bubble – as mentioned. My father would probably have commented on the proposal that everyone responds to a vacant space with an idea for how to use it creatively by saying: "Only true to a limited extent." I really admired him for that. A situation in which several approaches with different weightings can be the right one can be rhetorically solved without getting tangled up in things yourself and taking sides. That's pretty elegant. The question of what relationship one has to the issue of exhibiting in a space or even just imagining this, and what others think about that, is not something you answer as if facing a multiple-choice paper. Rather, this is essentially about a rhizome of possible approaches. Added to which, there are aspects which play a role that cannot be contemplated without pausing for a moment. For I suspect that the assumption that collecting art always also entails the wish to have your own museum halls – in other words, to erect a monument to yourself – actually involves a colorful bundle of feelings being brought into play that are otherwise frowned upon. Why resort to Hegel, to bring Grandma Josefine back into the argument, when ascribing such thoughts to the collectors? Why are the imagined (!) dreams of people you usually don't know in person and whom you have nothing to do with of interest anyway? Possibly the very idea that there is a "wishful feel" wherever you look, and that includes homes that house an art collection, is somehow soothing. Making the effort to imagine that people who can seemingly afford anything and everything do not manage to lay their hands on the one or other desirable byproduct seems somewhat quirky to me. I note with a small frog in my throat that this quirkiness is fairly widespread in the professional world in which I move.

Andrei Roiter N.Y.

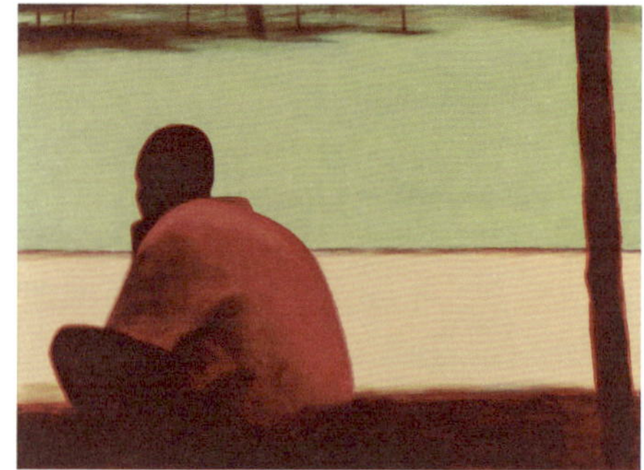

Andrei Roiter REFUGE

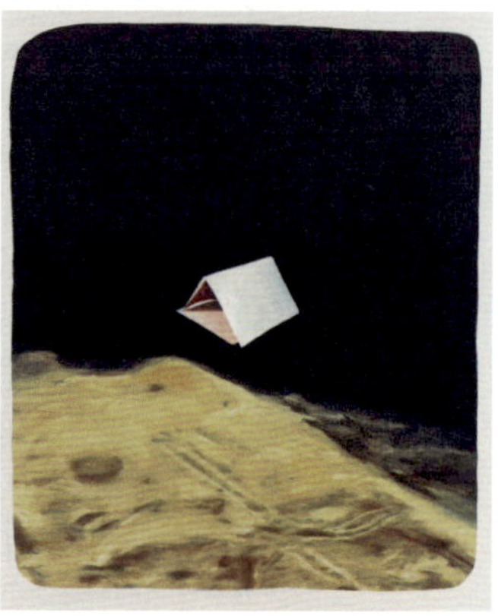

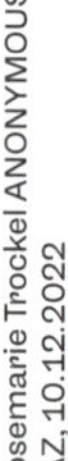

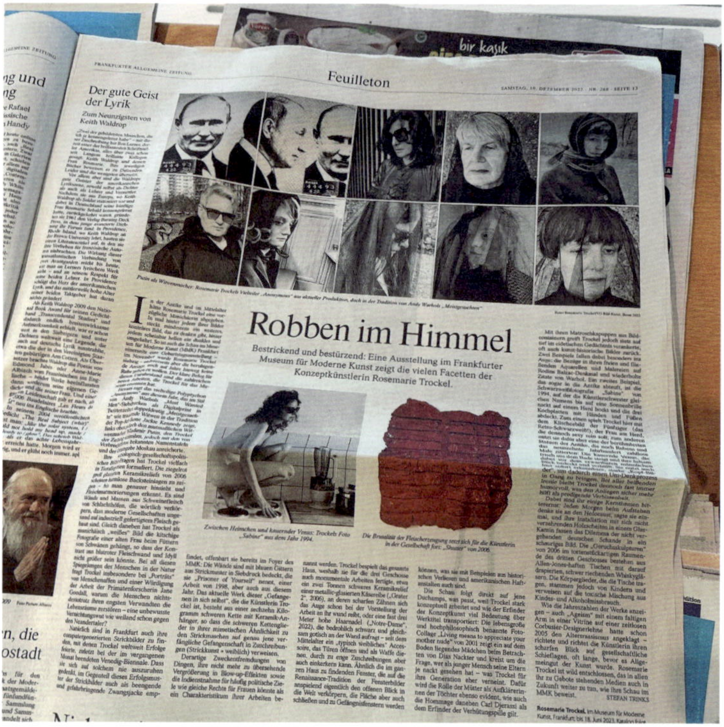

Feuilleton

Robben im Himmel

Bestrickend und bestürzend: Eine Ausstellung im Frankfurter Museum für Moderne Kunst zeigt die vielen Facetten der Konzeptkünstlerin Rosemarie Trockel.

Rosemarie Trockel ANONYMOUS, FAZ, 10.12.2022

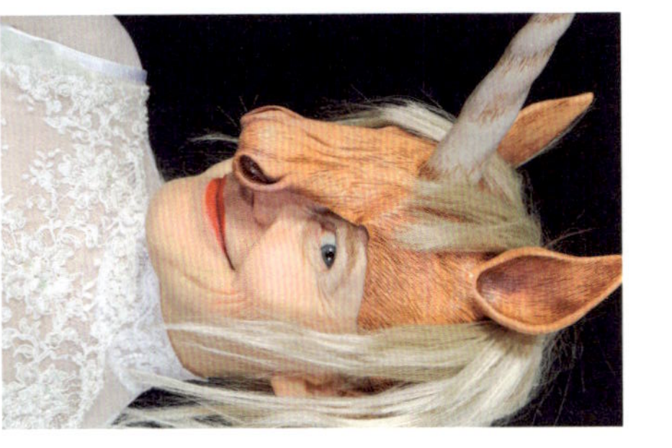

Claudia Holzinger
EINHORN (UNICORN)

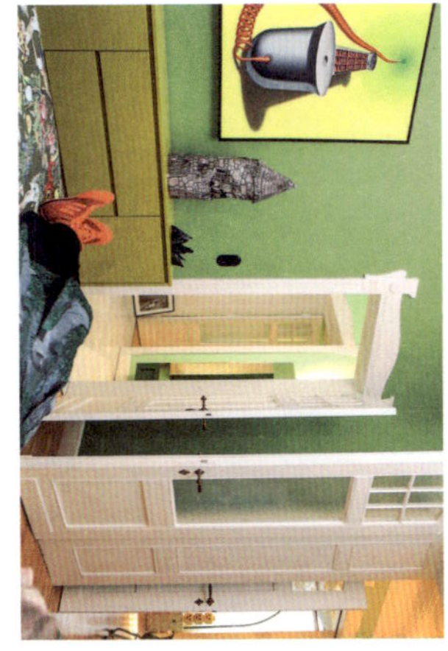

Konrad Klapheck, Claus Hugo Nielsen,
Nan Hoover, Arnold Odermatt
Photo: Bettina Fürst-Fastré

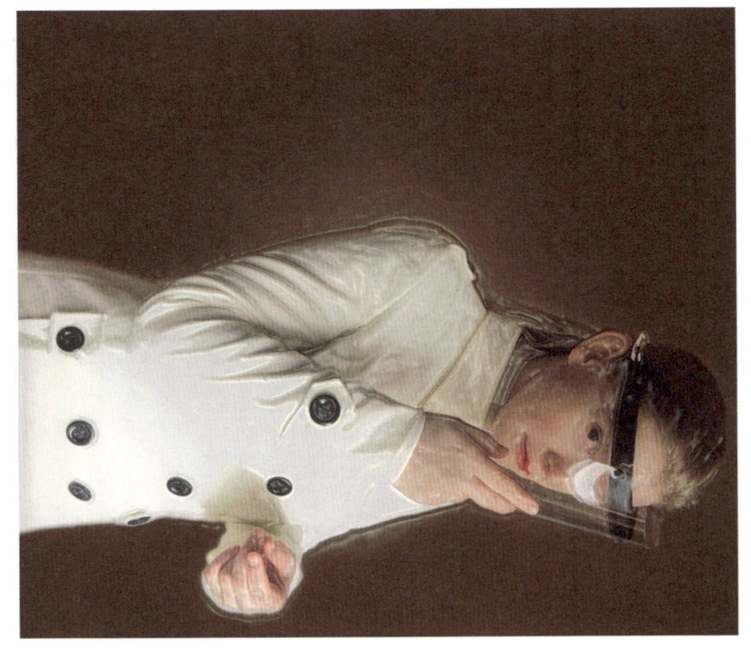

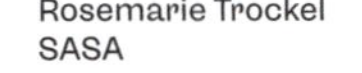

Rosemarie Trockel
SASA

Keeping up with the Joneses or straightforward sociology

Once I had noticed the fact, I started noticing it all the more often: Conversations with my clients centered in astonishingly great detail not on issues of their own, such as legal matters or strategic decisions relating to their own art, but more on the suspected motives of third parties. I find them explaining to me extensively who had what neurotic inclination to try and be seen as best and who sees what completely wrongly. They then always define their own position in contrast to that of the other players in the field of life where they are active together, but the tone, the indignation, and the defiance in such accounts at times really disconcert me. I lurk, awaiting the part when they say something that requires my expertise. What specialist question requires solving on behalf of this client sitting in front of me? What does the client actually want? Precisely this point, however, is often not even reached, and conversations get bogged down in opacity. As a lawyer and court-appointed expert, I then feel as though I am somehow playing the wrong role. The conversations move along as if I were a therapist or being employed to act as the person's coach. Predominantly, the conversation starts simply because the agreed appointment starts. My client meanders about without interruption. Now, while my clients don't lie on a couch, there is nevertheless almost no eye contact. We gaze out into space or toy with the coffee or teacups. In contrast to what one might expect in a specialist advisory setting, I do considerably less of the talking than does the client. On occasion, I provide impulses, but these impact neither on the content nor on the flow of talking. The clients' monolog regularly leads to déjà-vu, as I suddenly start thinking I have heard exactly the same text before. To be precise, the contributions do not sound to me "as if" I had heard them before, because the as-if is out of place; I have indeed heard them before, a few times, and down to the very last nuance. The clients report on their views with such verve and involvement that I have to assume they themselves doubtless have the impression that they are telling me something completely and utterly NEW. In my lectures at such points, I tend to quote the satirical sermon in Monty Python's Life of Brian. The Messiah, naked on a balcony, calls to the masses: "You are all individuals!" And the masses unanimously and gloriously reply: "Yes! We are all individuals!"

Déformation professionnelle

Despite the routine of many years in the profession, at some point I invariably need simply to interject and set things straight from my point of view. To be honest, I sometimes feel inclined, after so much long-winded navel-gazing in the milieu spread out before me, to wonder why on earth the clients are even on my couch (which is actually an armchair) if they already know everything better anyway. However, I decided a long time ago that it is best not to seem bitter. In the situation in question, I never discern an opportunity to present something that indicates my own perception of things and yet at the same time ensures that I remain above reproach. In other words, I lack not only the couch, but also the authority to hand down a diagnosis on a person's behavior. Perhaps this is a matter of professional deformation. Because before the court you carefully need to make very certain that you provide no fuel for concerns that you might be biased. If I judge behavior the way I would judge the quality of a lecture, then I would always seem to be involved, to have taken sides. Moreover, the setting has very strict parameters. First, I don't get a word in edgeways, and second, the clients provide the answers themselves: Of course, one is completely unlike all the others and the approach taken to one's own collection is unique, special, incomparable. Sometimes my consultation ends without a tangible problem, let alone one I could solve professionally, had this even been halfway mentioned. Then you need endurance. The era when you could enter "impatience" in the section for bad character traits in job applications in order to seem all revved up and ready for the new are long since over. Over time I've learned to listen to descriptions of what, to my mind, was only to be expected, without in any way judging this. It's simply like drinking a third beer. After only one glass I refuse to drive; it's no longer a matter of quenching thirst, but it won't leave me drunk. The third glass tastes simply like… the second glass; it's something familiar and it doesn't hurt. It is what it is. Enough is enough, however, as another glass will only taste bitter, and, three or four hours after being drunk, is still busy making itself felt. For the clients, this is evidently not as obvious as it is for me, namely since they are, statistically speaking, at the end of their lives, have children, own companies, houses, and a collection and need to put their affairs in order. The vague need to converse that brings (possible) clients to my law office seems to be like someone wanting to go to a shoemaker without taking the shoe that needs repairing along, in order, first of all, to discuss the pros and cons of a repair and then to talk in general about shoes to see whether this precise shoemaker is the right one. Needless to say, this conversation must not cost the client anything. I have not seen how this can be conveyed to clients. My conclusion? Possibly, the ability to be able to listen to the elaborate coloring in which an issue is clad for an indefinite period of time, and for such time to be paid time, is the most valuable of all professional experience. When I started my career, I thought that clients awarded you a job after a preliminary meeting. In actual fact, jobs arise from loose ties. I should have occupied myself more with sociology in days gone by. It would definitely have brought me a lot of time and considerably more income. Now I'm all the wiser.

Anyone making provisions for the future doesn't really need to do so

A recommendation from someone who is satisfied, or a tip from someone who reads either something by me or something about me, leads straight to my services being commissioned. Talks held to feel me out, described beforehand as "we need to sit down together", invariably result in navel-gazing and do not bring me bread and butter. Fundamentally, I meanwhile distrust all sentences in which there is talk of me "having to". "Having to" means responding to something else. Something has to be organized at long last, meaning someone doesn't have a last will, structures are not in place, and so on. Anyone who has made provisions, has got their life on track, doesn't "have to" do anything. And even worse in my eyes is combining the having to with a majority of the persons present – suddenly I'm supposedly part of the 100% of the "we have to". I respond about as favorably to that as I do to the overall issue of nuclear power. Profits are private and yet the problems are for everyone, now and in the future. The collector garners the success of a collection. The problems of a storeroom left unattended, in the worst case one encumbered by debates over restitution or authenticity, is something subsequent generations can solve. For a few years now, I have been carefully monitoring whether and when a collector speaks of "we" when the relevant players are "me, myself, and I". Collectors seek to avoid having to pay for advice as regards the art collection, specifically in connection with taxes and handing it on to the next generation. Accordingly, all too often the right point in time for advice that would really promise success tends to be missed. As a rule, people seek me out for advice once the cart has got truly stuck in the mud. In my first few years in the profession, I wanted to help others catch up on time lost. And I wanted to excel. Once I was awarded a contract, I always tried to cut to the chase quickly. I wanted to show I could fulfil the tasks swiftly and cost-effectively. I've long since shed that hubris. Because swiftly completed expert opinions are not held in high regard. Perhaps I would have been better off as a plumber. Or even as an emergency locksmith. Work requiring trivial skills but done at awful hours is paid handsomely in such professions, and you get extra praise if the door then pops open or the heating ramps back up. As a fast-working lawyer I got none of that – I was simply suspected of not being thorough. Not to mention that a solution presented in no time at all damages the clients' self-perception – that theirs are the most serious problems and can only be solved by a specialist with great effort.

Sub-complex problems are not elegant

In the art market, no one wants to have sub-complex problems. You therefore need to be highly sensitive when offering solutions to the problems, and this most definitely means adjusting your schedule accordingly. Today I am much better at biding my time, and I no longer feel unconditionally compelled in person to solve the situation. Moreover, I no longer get insulted, and that was most emphatically the trickier lesson to learn. There was a time years ago when I regularly got really annoyed, for example if the court did not inform me of the outcome of the case for which I had submitted an expert opinion. Once upon a time, I believed that anyone who explained something to me down to the tiniest of details clearly thought me stupid or that I had failed to do my homework. All of that dented my pride. Today I have become more modest. The lion's share of what was presented to me as the facts of the matter had absolutely zero to do with me, that I now understand. Specifically, people who never become clients but who, as described above, first want a get-to-know meeting, now exclusively get to know me from the vantage point of wanting me as their particular audience. No one in this configuration is in the slightest bit interested in my level-headed view of things, steeped as it is in a wealth of specialist experience. Indeed, excellent legal and expert approaches annoy people and disturb the relationship with clients, because they do not enable me to bring anyone on board.

Drama can't be allayed by law

As a result, I accept the role I need to play, and I also put up with the fact that, have I managed to get a word in edgeways, it may very well be repeated back to me in this or the very next conversation as the client's own thoughts. I have learned to see this as an advantage. Not just because the clock is ticking, but because predominantly the issues relating to a collection are described in such an overly complicated and anecdotally clichéd manner that from a specialist point of view, I can only be happy that the clients neither expect to nor accept advice. Given the abbreviated matter at hand, dressed up in all manner of colors, it would be all too easy to provide advice that could be contested or was downright wrong. I correspondingly listen to the same old chestnuts without passing comment, if only out of interest in myself. Inwardly I am counting the number of "yes but only if" iterations we have got through. Irrespective of how many communications seminars my clients have already attended as part of their job or for some honorary activity they perform – when it comes to art, they suffer a relapse. In other words, I get the impression of having extremely young individuals sitting opposite me. As regards the development of my own children, I learned in conversations on how well they were doing at school that there is a phase in life in which the rules are already known, and you simply cannot yet apply them to yourself. The phenomenon can crop up again later in life. This I now know. One variant of this inability to apply regularities and the rules of the game to oneself is the assertion that there is no solution for one's own problem. Whenever a possible solution is voiced, it is countered by a "but". Example: The successor generation is very interested in art, but they need to be guided. Of course, the inheritors should be free to do as they choose, but the collection must not be disbanded. Sure, one would like to… but the tax authorities. And, they continue, the world is full of collectors who don't love their art but are only interested in investments, whereas they put so much effort into the collection, assume responsibility. Like a mantra: "There is no solution!"

Pragmatism does not support the craving for importance

At any rate, the competition to possess the most intractable or (to stick with art terminology) one-off problem seems likewise pretty odd to me. I find myself being told how awful the client's childhood was, and every itchy pullover is explored to test its potential for boosting the ordeal one has to go through. Were not all pullovers itchy and didn't all sneakers stink after a while but a couple of decades ago? That said, this drama seems to have a value all of its own. This can't be countered by law and/or a pragmatic approach. Because pragmatism does not nurture the craving for importance, for prominence. The above-described phenomena are not the exclusive privilege of those who collect art. In the case of a company being passed on to the next generation, the same known standards come into play. What both the collector and the entrepreneur/company owner have in common is an inability to imagine a world without them. Just as collecting and entrepreneurialism are both linked to playing a game, the assumption is that specifically collecting rests on the motivation of denying death. The person involved accordingly finds it very difficult to imagine how others will live with the objects in question. The question as to life with a collection is therefore one that arises in general and can be answered likewise generally and independently of the object of the collection. There are many aggregations of objects. What to do with all the things belonging to the kids who have moved out, or with the objects bequeathed to us by parents, grandparents, aunts and uncles? The things left to us or abandoned to us are all bound up with the hi/stories of those who so liked them. Do we know these stories? Do we want to know these stories? Can there be new stories?

Collecting is a life lived in exuberance

In recent years there has been much public discussion on order, clearing up, throwing out clutter. Yet collecting means excess, not efficiency. Collecting is in part redundant and inherently not committed to reduction. Is clearing up and throwing out the clutter really the preferential means? Concerning oneself with a collection or, to put it neutrally, with a matter in its entirety, is like confronting antiquities. With the difference that the latter things exist. Fragments of the hi/stories have been passed down, but the actual historical scope largely remains in the dark and beyond access. In the case of household items (however precious they may be), the aspect of use always remains. A Rolex, a Meissner tableware set, a bureau. A shoulder shrug as regards the external appearance and the price purportedly paid way back when always play a role, but the item's actual purpose, its use, remains. In the case of art objects, by contrast, which by definition have no practical use, it's easy to find it difficult to come up with an explanation. Why was that bought in the first place? Why does one particular work hang prominently in the public part of the home or behind the principal's desk (see Wolfgang Ullrich, Mit dem Rücken zur Kunst. Die neuen Statussymbole der Macht, [With your back to art. The new status symbols of power, Berlin, 2000]) and why is another piece at the very back in the storeroom, stood facing the wall? What strikes me with every ostensible "attic find" greeted enthusiastically in the press and every collection put on show is that such individual cases compare with countless unspectacular inheritances that the subsequent generation spends ages digesting emotionally and silently away from the public razzmatazz. Is the energy that was devoted to a collection then lost? Yes, of course I know that energy can't get lost. Put differently: Why does a collection or an artist's estate enter into entropy? When, in contrast to this, does a portfolio get focused such as to garner success and become well-known? For a variety of reasons, I for one during the crucial years in my professional life did not ever have the "luxury problem of a collection". In my family no one died. My parents' house was so large that after I moved out, for ages nothing happened until I couldn't care what they did with the remnants of my adolescence.

Keeping a diary s like studying aw

I always recorded in diaries anything that was important to me. Leafing through a diary many years on is emotionally potentially draining. The one or other judgment, be it positive or negative, is hard to digest. Shame and irritation bubble up in me when I read incisive lines about people whom I have completely forgotten. That said, the benefits and joy outweigh the downside. Today I have far better knowledge of people and the ability to discern motives and patterns, and predict actions instead of being caught cold, and I attribute this in large part to the constant self-inquiry down through the decades. Although the number of diaries has since topped 90, they still all fit in two removal crates and disappear (wherever they have arrived) into a cupboard. In the course of the ages, and depending on the social context, writing a diary was considered poetic, anal-compulsive, or vain. Like studying law, for me writing a diary is a very useful technique for getting through life. Both lead to me knowing things better. The notions that third parties have of women who keep diaries or study law, meaning Jane Austen on the one hand and buying a Barbour jacket on the other, invite caricature, humorous comment, and coarse jokes. Saying to someone that you curse them, that you would inflict pain on them – now that sounds like megalomania and movies, the ones I don't watch. I gladly evoke the idea that this will land in my black notebook – forever and ever. That fear and that invitation to take the front seat in everything. Why? Because it works? When I started writing, long before I graduated from high school, I basked in the literary mannerism that a large swath of my social circle considered it to be, without being able to put my finger on it. It did not take long for me to become relatively proficient in keeping a diary. At the one level, I was always aware that inner growth and a productive angle on the world can only be achieved not by wishing for them but by adopting suitable habits. I've always been wary of crash courses and hyper-fast diets. Whenever someone says that she is motivated, the inner governess in me says: "Well, let's wait and see." Way back when, I found it difficult to communicate this inner focus, whereas today you can find it in any self-improvement paperback. I usually liked being considered a bit of a nutty eager beaver who took her own life so utterly seriously that she kept a diary on it. The very idea that I was able to retain control of how my own life was interpreted was something I found calming and healthy. After all, I grew up in a setting in which people were of the opinion I didn't want to have a family of my own and was primarily interested in pursuing a career. The diary was and is a protected space in order to model possible paths through life. Both studying law and keeping a diary encourage one to produce text. You only learn to write by writing. In the course of time, I found out that even highly educated and eloquent persons can often not write. Correspondence remains untouched and projects cannot take off because the exposé that is supposed to whisk everyone off their feet cannot be written. That is constraining. Among people whom I meet in the art business, one phenomenon resulting from this limitation plays a hefty role. If you cannot express yourself on paper, you tend to take a dim view of others who manifestly can write and/or do so. In Operating System Art this actually means that since they themselves do not publish, or what they do churn out is not what they would like it to be, they are prone to self-deprecation and humbling in connection with publications about them. As soon as an opportunity to appear on a piece of paper pops up, as soon as someone switches on a Dictaphone, such people start talking two to the dozen. What I have observed is that these publications – and they simply invite one to feel ashamed for the person in question – are less a matter of shameless exhibitionism and more of the absence of the healthy intimacy that a diary can offer. I think one pragmatic alternative approach here would be to rely on a ghost writer.

Long live the division of labor, I say!

Because usually human abilities are limited. The all-round genius, the golden goose, is a mythical beast. Just because a person is a talented or committed artist does not mean they are suited to be a press spokesperson or essayist. We all laugh about how, come the World Cup, just about everyone in the room is a professional referee. Remarking that the same people are not interior designers, art experts, or housekeepers tends to fall on deaf ears. What I find most impertinent is when people say to my face that they'll simply become cleaners if they don't get the job. As if everybody can be as good a cleaner as those other persons who are paid to clean. A distinguishing characteristic of great giftedness to my mind is therefore the ability to recognize one's own limits and to focus on what one has sufficient potential in, instead of playing the amateur expert in all sorts of different fields. So, no Aikido for me, no, my thing is to let the letters do the fighting. As a young woman, since to be honest, there was not in fact always something original about myself to reflect on in my diary, and my imagination was for the same reason limited, I often wrote for others. Love letters, for example. Later speeches for exhibition previews, tricky responses, this and that. Writing love letters for other people is truly wonderful. The emotions are there. Actors can't portray anything, after all, which is not rooted somewhere in their range of experiences. Or at least that's how I imagine acting to be. Writing a love letter on my own behalf, now that is as difficult as taking the floor in court as a lawyer in a law suit you have yourself brought. The relevant term here is the worry that you need to declare an interest. Sadly, the division of labor doesn't work in many places in society today. Because there's no structured market for many of the very useful tools in life. An established market, a trading place, an exchange for buying and selling the most important things for your life does not, as far as I know, exist. Love is not something that needs a declaration. The possible child of the chip-eater from Berlin has little prospect of emotionally settled parents. Romance needs a shape and a vocabulary. I had my reflexes under control and did not give in to the impulse to turn my head. I definitely did not bark at the ladies: Your problem trance is pretty damn unsexy. After all, they were busy saying more about themselves than about Benny. Perhaps this particular Benny is a pretty good bloke. No, that's just nonsense, too. I smack my wrist for my social romance. At one level, I realize that my aloofness from the real world is doubled up here, as I can afford social romance. Reality is a long way off. So long live the protective space afforded by boarding school, by studying, and by whiling away time in the art milieu. Well, yes, fortunately, wherever it may come from, you need a little talent, too. The diary in my handbag was, at any rate, the signal to my surroundings that well-compiled excerpts from the same could be used for any number of purposes. Here a marriage newly forged, there a column in print. I spent my school internship with one of the bigger dailies, and the editor-in-chief felt that anyone could write about summer sales, but what he really needed was a few new glosses. "The readers want to smile. Why not sift through your diaries?" Now those were all really beneficial dummy runs and assuaged my fear of the white sheet in front of me, of putting pen to it with thoughts. It is from writing that I have my respect for what a fine artist achieves, but to a certain extent also for all entrepreneurial figures who create something that did not exist before. For me, writing a love letter or being a fine artist are comparable. Both focus on your own inner world, exposed and vulnerable, visible from afar, and prone to quotation. Something similar applies to entrepreneurs. They dare to try and do something – and are therefore exposed to public criticism and run the risk of failure. Should they be successful, then they also need to be able to handle that. Is this a possible explanation for the disappearance of the entrepreneurial spirit? The diary is most certainly a good place for one to keep the private persona separate from the public iteration and to consider what the outside world should preferentially not be exposed to. Under the sign of irritation, when I reread passages in the diary what strikes me is that people and situations that heralded what, in retrospect, were key turning points or serve as the material for especially nice anecdotes, and yet back then, when first committed to the diary, I wrote about them in a very sober idiom given the acuteness of the matter. While I am writing, I already know that I will reread these lines in a few weeks and in a few years. The conscious description for internal use is straightforwardly the initial attempt to record the facts, while the assessment only arises over time. The diary is, in other words, a place where you practice, where you get ready to launch into life. Collecting is often a similar readying to embrace life, and entrepreneurs who are collectors are testing themselves and the world. As said, game theory explains this behavior by approximation. Game theory sounds comical as a term. Thinking seriously about playing games. Which is also a serious affair. For that reason, there's little laughter on the football pitch or in the game of love. Or is there?

Objects of affection

For many years, there were no objects of affection in my life. The number of artworks I had accumulated was also minimal. The art I owned was more proof of my work, the way trophies and medals are in sport. I first noticed how collectors tussle inwardly with the art they already possess and desire to own other pieces, to own more, but I never really thought about it. I only peripherally noticed the manifestly real pain of those involved in Operating System Art – like the guests waiting at the gate or the mustard jar in the fridge door. The observations didn't trigger anything in me. Clearly, I was not able to follow any of this emotionally. I did not delve into this pain because I did not even understand the underlying structure: Why commit so many resources (money, time, dedication) for results that were not the ones desired? After all, you don't assemble a personal collection because you have to. Why take up a hobby that doesn't, at the end of the day, make you happy? It's that trivial? If you've already opted for the role of collector, why tussle inwardly with things? Instead of looking to the left or right or rather upwards to the heavens, why not commit all that energy to the matter itself in order to make certain the collection is good in your eyes and makes you feel good? Taking a position in relation to others always seems about as joyless to me as speculating about the emotional world of others. I consider myself an essentially inquisitive person. I find other people especially interesting. I'm quite superficial when I enjoy people-watching, when they walk past my office or float past on a scooter, the way they phone, eat an ice-cream, or talk to their children. I like being astonished by the bartender's timing. With what a leisurely touch you can always keep even a small "kitchen" in the best of order and produce something at the drop of a hat. Such scenes get seared into my memory as if I had seen a really major auteur film; indeed, if nothing else is going on, such as when I'm waiting for an airplane or until the machine has finished gurgling and has produced my coffee, I rerun these movies before my mind's eye. The guttural laughter of a girlfriend who is pouring me a cup of tea, the downcast gaze of a friend running his hand through his hair, and the newspaper seller carefully rolling up an issue for a client and raising an eyebrow when calculating the price in his head. This is what the world is like, structured by well-rehearsed routines that exude inner peace and security. As long as I do not hear anything to the contrary, I assume everything is in order. In other words, I approach the world in an inconceivably undramatic way. The statement that there's an old soul in me initially seemed strange. If there is such a thing, then it probably does apply to me and I gaze at the big wide world through the eyes of my ancestors, who were farmers. Much is simply a given, like the weather, the seasons, and you live with that not in opposition to it, and trying to speed things up, be it with fertilizers or greenhouses, always comes at a price. Every individual activity is important; at the same time, you can't force things; yet every day's piece starts with a first step. It was not until I worked in the art business that I realized: In that sphere there are an increasing number of completely different ways of approaching the world. If the intended success does not occur immediately, then people start suspecting that dark forces are at work everywhere, and everyone is then always busy because they are invariably short-staffed. Not just in collections and studios, but also in museums, I increasingly encounter the underlying mood that nothing is essentially well positioned and that each and every individual seems to be dissatisfied. Is that the invariable price for playing out a bit part in a celebrity market?

Don't worry, be happy

Something is out of kilter here. Why are so many people busy betting if the people with money are apparently all frightened that others like them because of their money and not because of their inner virtues? Why is the number of cosmetic surgical interventions forever climbing if people who would normally be considered beautiful purportedly have the problem that they don't know whether they are loved for their hearts or only desired for their appearance? What if there is no one single rule or truth and one can do it this way or that way? What, or so I sometimes want to ask, if there are people who don't bother themselves with whether they are loved but simply accept it with great joy as a gift without asking questions? Isn't this the phenomenon known as complete trust? So, what if the dangerously high Cinderella shoes don't cause corns? What if imagined, over-privileged people feel like bugs in a rug as part of the jet-set and do not want a deep-frozen pizza and self-prepared vegan dish in their house at the end of the terrace? Whenever I get caught up in such a conversation about the life and feelings of the imagined icons of the art and celebrity market, words such as "class blindness", "keeping up with the Joneses", or "social romance" get bandied about, and I find everything very simple and at the same time very complex. Since becoming responsible for a collection myself, I sometimes notice how my heart races: What if someone now asks me directly? After all, I am myself one of these privileged sample models. But it never happens. Present company is always excepted from these considerations. Those involved do not, as a matter of principle, get asked such things directly, let alone substantively. For a while, I thought that people did not perceive me as being a member of the relevant circles and instead still viewed me as a curator or something similar, and in such a discourse it is only the views of "those involved" that count. That, too, does not seem to apply. Because the selfsame people who object that I cannot possibly understand their specific, difficult situation without batting an eyelid then introduce me to third parties as a collector.

Since I had experienced this again and again down through the years, it gradually dawned on me what it is that collectors' kids mean when they complain that in their parental homes persons from the outside were always more important than they were. The children were admonished to behave properly, but any old artists who tipped up at the front door were suddenly puffing away on a cigarette in the living room and got away with whatever scurrilous behavior they so liked. The kids had not been allowed to go skiing as cash was tight, and at the same time unbelievable sums were shelled out in galleries and studios because "it's important". The fact that, in many cases, after a short while these very images are as good as worthless, and the buyer wants absolutely zero to do with the artist any longer, is something the children often find deeply satisfying. It's more important to the children that their parents' fuss about art was nonsense than that their deprivations back then paid off in dollars and cents. Collectors' children often part company with their parents as regards their need for material truth. That they felt the treatment back then to be unjust they then considered to be true to this day.

A world in rumor mode

Art market players actually don't want to know many things particularly intricately. Seen in this light, the opaqueness of the art market does not appear to be so much a problem, but rather fertile ground for the imagination. Accordingly, the fairy tales of today flourish in the murky circles of art. There, the talk is of art lovers who have morphed into gentleman thieves. These commissioned thieves of passion are a bit like Jack the Ripper. Everyone's heard of him, everyone knows this or that about him, but no one knows for certain who he was. Anyone drawn under the magic spell of the art market seems to indulge in notions of mysterious machinations, legendary wealth, and thus the invariable related dark sides. Even the legislative seems to be influenced by erroneous ideas about the art world and senses money laundering wherever it looks. If I were to rely for my information solely on what people tell me in my own law office, then seen from the worm's eye view everyone in the art market must be battling with dissatisfaction at the roles they actually play.

Men are geniuses women diligent

After all, unfulfilled dreams are falsely attributed not just to collectors. Rather, there is a blanket assumption that everyone involved in art somehow wanted to be different. Artists are often spared because they move outside the bounds of bourgeois society anyway, and to foster an inner distance they can be assumed to have gone unnoticed for a very long time, to have lived in bitter distress, or simply to be charlatans. Female artists are not spared because it is assumed they would have had a far easier time of things if they had been men and would thus logically prefer to be men. Any talk of gender justice is irrelevant here. Here and there the language is gendered and there is something like a quota, but when push comes to shove, everything remains the same. The dust raised over non-binary gender positions, so it goes, serves only to divert attention away from the market constants. I would translate these purported constants as follows: Men are geniuses, women are diligent. Which is why men are more expensive. Less has always been paid for diligence, because in art what counts is the IDEA. Meaning that those who move in the art market, for example as journalists or in event management, have basically missed the boat and not become artists or gallerists in time. For their part, gallerists would prefer to be museum folk, and all the critics would ostensibly prefer to be exhibition makers, while curators would just love to be collectors with a big budget at hand, and so on and so forth, the one a greater tragedy than the next. Have I read too much Andreas Reckwitz and therefore am surprised? For does Reckwitz not say that the problem can be solved by a symbiosis of your own bourgeois focus on status with the yearning for Romantic self-actualization to achieve truly successful self-actualization? (The Society of Singularities, [Polity: Cambridge, 2020], p. 207) One well-known pattern: Why does one not act logically? Why does no one do their homework? Tax returns, living wills, last will and testament, and cancelled subscriptions, or precisely the right choice of profession, are for adults what homework is for kids. In Operating System Art, that could possibly function, that combination of self-realization and the satisfaction of status cravings. Pseudo-feudal positions such as museum director, big-time gallerist, or celebrated artist should surely fit the bill. Has no one noticed this? There would appear to be no space for happy, satisfied odd-ones-out who have done their homework. Evidently that is not a genre that is on people's radar when they think about the art world. Dissatisfied and driven – that is what the characters in it are supposed to be. To my ears, that sounds antiquated.

Pattern ABC at schoo[l] and in Operatin[g] System Ar[t]

Just like notions regarding vacant properties, the feeling of isolation as something essentially advantageous has accompanied me throughout my life. What strikes me is that among those around me, something is handled in a way that I simply find wrong. I never found it cool to suddenly panic shortly before exams or holidays. Recently, someone coquettishly said that they were chaotic. Somewhat at a loss, I tried to keep my face as neutral as possible. Because my propensity for sincerity should actually have forced me to disagree. Why should less output, a lost notion of the bigger picture, and disorganization be an advantage? Many people clearly see things differently. The sticker claiming "A genius masters chaos" does not convey much of a joke. How often has someone said that to me by way of an explanation for the fact that a piece of work was incomplete, and I should please wait a little longer until the genius of a chaotic person has worked its magic? I don't like thinking such moments through, as here we have someone claiming to be a genius and at the same time manifestly implying that my insistence on the clarity of order means I am most definitely not a genius. My socialization does not fit things at this juncture. My education in a convent boarding school taught me more that "inner and outer order" lead to the desired results. There was no talk of genius. And not because I attended a girl's school; no, the nuns believed we could even move mountains. In the art market, people simply do not believe that a structured approach leads to you reaching your goal. An artist has to be a genius, and a career must always be some inexplicable

Jenny Holzer PROTECT ME FROM WHAT I WANT
Olaf Holzapfel (hay object), Angela Glajcar → 102

miracle. At the same time, people expect that everyone in the art market is somehow inwardly driven, as otherwise they would of course not have enough passion for things. Which is to say that knowledge, ability, and structured activity always have to be applied in the right doses.

The term "eager beaver" is unfair to animals

If you paid attention at school, then you'll know what the doses need to be. Because in handling teachers, it always seemed to me beneficial to get the dosing right. Anyone who refuses to listen to the teacher is not about to be liked by the person who is at the front of the class. Meaning I don't know everything better, but quite officially study hard as supervised by the teacher in class. That's the one part of it. At the same time, it was intuitively clear to me that I was in danger. Because what would happen if I didn't make progress on my own? I really couldn't bring myself to trust those who praised me for everything I was able to do, what with not having gone to kindergarten and being lightyears ahead of the curriculum at school. Didn't these people notice that I was concerned? I had the impression of being left to my own resources. What if I wasn't able to teach myself something? Observing other kids, I was able to note that they first made a big deal out of being bored and then missed the right point to enter the fray again. When is the right point to enter things, if you haven't learned how to study in a structured manner? How do the self-taught (kids) manage the transition? Why is the first day at school or the high-school graduation party such a big deal when there are so many hassles in between? Or is there some other explanation as to why an astonishingly large number of people who have graduated with higher degrees are helpless or apathetic when it comes to tasks relating to law or taxes or "old-age provisions"? If saving money is associated with a piggy bank and money is otherwise a tabooed subject, then simply buy NFTs. As a substitute activity. As a smaller child, I was consequently a bit sulky and actually always worried. At boarding school, meaning at the start of high school, that improved. Because my questions no longer went unanswered, but in cases of doubt teachers and educators found people who could be presented without much ado with my questions and who provided answers. At the same time, the teachers wittily and quite originally went about training me in humility. I was expected to help the other children and, if necessary, even allow them to have a sneak-peak at my answers. It "will not cost you anything to help." I had to learn to nurture the weaker pupils, as this would be good for my soul. My mother sent me off to boarding school with the idea that everyone in boarding school was a paying student and I wouldn't be responsible for the success of others. For her, being alone way out in front made sense. That was to remain a bone of contention between us till the end of her life. The Franciscans who ran the school had other ideas. The success of the other girls that we achieved with great effort together was more precious to me than my own, essentially shock-free, progress in class.

So much for "whoopee"

At times, I was moving along in what for me was an ideal state: no wunderkind and no oddball, but fruitfully engaging with the world. However, my launch into the world of education at primary school still pops up in my dreams. From day one, I had the vague impression that the place was not there for me but that, conversely, I had to do something for the people there. Although it was pretty hard to establish what exactly. At any rate, you had to always appear happy. If I started the day subdued, my mother would often pronounce stridently to me that:

"Whoopee, I'm a school pupil and no longer small." And I don't even think she was being cynical. Most people were evidently unable to imagine that children can do something really well without liking it. I hated primary school, and the way I saw it, all the other people there were completely insane. In other words, I somehow felt my cohort needed to be pitied and were most definitely and nastily unpredictable. Because I was considered a goody-two-shoes, I had to sit next to the toughies. And they attended irregularly and with no preparations. If they had a letter of apology for their absence from their parents or bandages round their heads, then it was because they had fallen out of the bunkbed at home or had been playing with the power socket and got a shock. Q. e. d.: insane and unpredictable. The teacher, her make-up so thick as to resemble a mask, rewarded us for good marks with candy. Sometimes she even gave us little pieces left over from Sunday's cake-bake. For every good answer, a bit was placed straight on your tongue. A circus performance it was. Welcome to the performing seals. She was effusively happy if we showed our thanks. I don't like butter-cream cake. I don't have a sweet tooth. I was brave and grasped that I was responsible for making certain that the teacher enjoyed a precious experience of her own effectiveness in successfully teaching me something. Years later, I was grateful for a few books by Elfriede Jelinek and invented a formulation for the mood that this setting evoked in me: Today, I'm Thomas Bernhard all day. Too complicated? A one-off? I don't think so. Because I encounter comparable things here and there. Somewhere along the line, things falter in the service society. Housekeepers need praise and recognition – fishing for compliments. Today, one would probably say "fishing for respect". Anyone wanting to be Housekeeper of the Week does the following: In the unloading of a dishwasher, a piece of tableware is simply placed on the cooktop instead of being cleared away. In dusting or vacuuming, a few things get rearranged, everything is somehow positioned slightly differently. It is not even necessary to do something special, meaning something in the direction of cleaning. Specifically, curtains provide a superb means of communicating with the employer. You simply pull the curtains a little more closely together or further apart. The main thing is: change. Just as the turn-down service in the hotel makes the bed appear slightly different, so I already know: Someone was here, someone provided a service.

Housework is work that you don't see when it's been done

My notion that housework you delegate to someone else in exchange for remuneration is work that you don't see when it's been done is evidently not shared by all. If I am by chance there at the time when the housework is being done, I experience something that is very similar to what I call the phenomenon "Grandma's going to make you a jam sandwich". In this case, the piece of tableware is placed on the cooktop, but if you're present then there is text added to give the scene color, and quite a lot of it. When I was a child, it was already inexplicable to me that the grandmothers of other kids said to their grandchildren: "Grandma's going to make you a jam sandwich," thus assisting them by providing this simple meal. What is it about the situation that prompts this commentary? Why does the grandmother not teach the child how to make a jam sandwich and instead does it occasionally, standing at a table with a quite unnatural posture? I guess I come from another world.

Education means making oneself superfluous

My grandmother smoked fish. She filleted a fish slowly, and then it was my turn for the next fish. That's what I knew. Education means making oneself superfluous, and service is making oneself invisible. My grandmother was able to kill a chicken and pluck it, and she showed me how eggs evolve inside a chicken. A string of eggs is like a film still. The frozen action impressed me. Today, performative photography is now a key part of the collection. If I see a film, then what went before it in time has already passed. In the case of photo sequences, I always have the entire action, the development, before my eye, and my mind can fill in what occurs between the photos. The works encourage you to think about what went before and what comes after. Individual film stills, by their nature, function differently because embedding them in a probable action is harder and at the same time always more open-ended. Whenever someone today says to me that these photographs are "only" a documentation of a performance and possibly do not really count as "artworks", I think "how pathetic". I go for a walk in these images, sometimes get lost when they cut too close to the quick, and the stories are frightening.

In the case of the string of eggs, I liked the fact that after insights were gained the object of investigation could be eaten. At the end of the day, performances, whose object is waste and destruction, are somehow uncanny to my mind. You might find this slightly anal compulsive of me and a little bit off the mark in terms of the subject matter, as art is by definition devoid of purpose, and everything material that is used in art remains bound to this freedom from purpose. Discussions about sustainability in art production

Gabriele Stötzer
TRANS VOR- UND ZURÜCKDREHEND
(TRANS TURNING FORWARD AND BACKWARD) → 102

seem to me on occasion somewhat overly agitated; in places, however, they get through to me. Mystery plays, battles with food, self-injury – these are unlikely to find their way into my collection. Here, I like the freedom in setting up and/or in my case continuing an existing collection. Instead of entropy, I discern the opportunity to weigh things up, take careful decisions, and choose freely how far I go along with a direction in art. Killing a chicken or the slaughtering that likewise took place on the farmyard do not persecute me in my dreams. Extracted from a significant context in my own life, in an exhibition in downtown Munich I once spontaneously vomited in a Nitsch show. I felt deeply ashamed of myself and yet found my response a healthy one. Perhaps, I thought, I am closer to the artist than the other visitors who all view it with cool superiority and managed during the private view to wolf down the finger-food and drinks. I find it an advantage that art touches me deeply and can shock me to the core. Over the years, I have learned to avoid the extremely shocking art experiences and to make certain I do not get persuaded to engage in confrontations with art that I will not easily endure. Needless to say, that doesn't always work. The more famous an art position, the more the audience is expected to be familiar with the oeuvre and be professionally hardened as regard the content. When I visited a Louise Bourgeois exhibition, I did so assuming I was well acquainted with the pictorial language. How wrong I was. I had to vomit and for the following two days felt seasick. The ground seemed to wobble beneath my feet, and I felt sick to my stomach. Despite these at times shocking experiences, I am grateful to feel things this way. I don't want to be cold and hard-nosed. Why concern yourself with something that doesn't get under your skin or (worse still) repeatedly shows you how hard a shell you have erected around yourself? In art and in love, shocks to the normal order of things are the clear objective. Here, agitation and a loss for words, uncertainty and an emotional vortex are completely in place. But not in the kitchen.

Lower forms of work as meaningful rituals

The considered calm with which my grandmother operated her wood-fired oven is exemplary for me. In the art business, you have to be well-traveled and culturally educated in order to have a weighty voice in the interpretative loops. Thus, when people get together, you spread your cultural knowledge – preferably acquired on highly individual trips abroad – out before you like a street vendor's carpet. On an evening with my friend Dominik, a Catholic priest, a famous female artist once mentioned all manner of exotic, meditation-suffused activities. Tea ceremonies, temples, the list was seemingly endless. When the meal was served, she and her husband immediately started eating. They almost indignantly laid down their spoons when we others started saying grace. My grandmother was a prophet in her own home, I thought to myself. Meditative immersion in myself was something I knew from the clinking of the rings on which the pots were positioned over the fire, and from the dishes simmering seemingly for all eternity on the oven that were then pushed around by the skillful movements her hands made among the pots and pans. And what indeed is a green tea compared to a meal prepared by my grandmother? When standing at the stove, I slip into the persona of my Grandma Klara. An additional dimension was added to this role decades ago, when the one hundred Deutschmark note came out bearing the head of Clara Schumann. Cooking is all about timing, dramaturgy, and energy. And playing the piano also means refusing to be hectic. The secret of Schumann's success was her carefully dosed approach, involving, at times, her playing with very great energy. Everything thus got mixed.

If I were to have a girl, she would be called Klara. With a C or with a K is something I would decide at a later date. In this way, I was always a strange, dazzling white child in my thoughts and for outside parties I assume, a girl who followed her grandparents like a shadow and soaked up everything they did like a sponge. No turn of the wrist went unnoticed. The twig of dill cut seemingly casually that helped produce the unforgettable salad dressing, the energetic wrist that grabbed the chicken that had sneaked into the vegetable garden, and the trajectory the chicken then took back into the poultry enclosure, the careful closing of the lid on the sauerkraut barrel in the cellar. In the large farm garden, there were also a few feathery strawberry plants. The fruits were the size of the powdery blueberries in supermarkets today. No doubt, preparing these pea-sized strawberries required much patience and skill. At the time, as I watched my grandmother using a small sharp knife to remove the little green tops off the strawberries, there was no indication that this was a truly big deal. Since men have started cooking at insular kitchens, I have heard a lot of the arduous nature of preparing a meal. From pregnant pauses to what are, to my mind, always far too intimate sighs and accentuated words – they all seek to make me notice what is being prepared for me here with great effort. “For me” is a turn of phrase that triggers me like all other formulations in which I and the word “must” crop up. A roommate, a cultured woman with a good feel for delicious food, came back from having dinner with a man, sat down on my sofa, and while I was still folding the newspaper away, she said something that immediately entered my active vocabulary: “I would have preferred to sit on the sofa and eat a pot meal.” Meaning it is an open issue who is being cooked for. It is not effort per se that decides the success, but the right effort. Sighs and laments did not exist in my grandmother’s kitchen. In my memory, my grandparents, as a matter of principle, spoke very little. Imitation sounds as communication, such as “sigh”, “ooof”, and “bam” were something on children’s TV programs and in comics, and I found them pretty exaggerated. In my real life, things were made and at some point, were finished and ready. Accordingly, at some point the enamel bowl was filled with miniature strawberries without their green hats, and these were then distributed over the cake base that had just been baked. They were then covered in red icing, which was what my grandmother called the liquid gummy bear coating. I felt the notion of icing was a little exaggerated here, as it was basically just glaze. Cakes with icing looked completely different, did they not? That my grandmother used a specialist term, and there were paper sachets in which the granulate for precisely this glaze was sold, was something I didn't find out until much later in life. The reality check for such things remains an issue in my life. Since I rarely shop, I have as good as completely retained my childish enthusiasm and the ability to be seriously surprised by what supermarkets have to offer. In this regard, I am as little hard-nosed as I am in art. The glaze took a while to set. And that timespan was exactly the amount of time Grandma needed to tip the strawberry hats out of her apron pocket and into the hen's bucket, clean the kitchen utensils by hand, and put everything away. She then took the coffee off the hob, which in the afternoon turned grey when she added a shot of milk, and the cake layer with the fruit was ready to be eaten, still slightly warm. I hardly eat any fruit now. Why should I, after all? I've already enjoyed the taste to the full, so what could there still be?

Elementary pedagogics

The silent skills of my grandparents were my elementary pedagogics. The stenciled figures that the kindergarten kids carry home, their hands all smeared by felt tips – that all seems dismal to me. Added to which, I find kindergarten kids stressed. They've constantly got appointments. The first few years of my life were an ocean of time. I can't remember being bored, in fact there seemed to be no place in my life for boredom. Was that a product of the fact that being stressed was something frowned upon in my early years? The condition under which I was allowed to spend time with my grandparents was "not to fidget about". They tolerated me because I was well-versed at adopting their rhythm. My granddad was a gruff man who consciously spoke little. His hands looked like branches. Sometimes, while I was in the middle of doing something, he wordlessly stroked my head with one of those frying-pan-sized hands, from the top of my head via an ear down to almost under my chin. Didn't say a word. No drama. We walked through his forests; he always had tools with him and there was something he needed to do. Here and there a bench in a clearing or a free seat, evidently specially for him. An ensemble of seating that to this day serves hikers as a resting place even bears his name. We would sit down, look at the soft rolling hills and listen to the birds. I let my legs swing in the air. Usually, he would magic a pear or a small apple out of a little basket or one of his huge trouser pockets, peel it, and give me small segments. A bonding, holy ritual. My grandparents thus together ensured my final, definitive exit from the fruit business. Grandma with her strawberries and Grandpa with his fruit. In spring, my grandfather dug out some moss in the woods, tied it up in a box with a piece of coarse string, and we carried it home together. In the garden, he then shaped an Easter egg nest for me under the cherry tree. Fine willow rods formed a roof structure that was covered with moss. One year, snow fell on Easter Sunday. For me, that was a sensation. Because the region in southwest Germany where I grew up is renowned for its sunny, mild climate, and even back in my childhood there was not much snow. So, the roof was not a toy roof but actually protected my Easter goodies. Decades later, in Hong Kong, I stood at a floor-to-ceiling hotel window with tears in my eyes, reminded by the trade-fair hall roof opposite of that Easter. Those were silent, precious moments with my grandfather. As a young person, I wasn't able to share these thoughts about him with anyone. In the family, his standing was that of the gruff old man. I was his favorite and "only topic" and thus, only naturally, was also given the status of the odd one out and was, at the very least, not taken seriously. Outside the family, there was no one I could have spoken with about my grandfather. He basically never left the farmyard. When my children were smaller, I stroked their heads the way he had mine, as if I wanted to smooth something on their heads. And I don't find myself odd if I do not leave the house, but wallow pleasantly in the memory. Which bonds. That way, I learned with my eyes and through imitation. Blabbering questions and comments were definitely not in order. All my cousins could have had a fruitful relationship with my grandparents, or so I already thought as a small child. If only they had not been so chatty! I liked being at my grandparents and even staying overnight. I found the space under the heavy clouds of the duvet between them a very safe place. The best moments of all were the minutes in which I had already taken my place between them and could watch how, as sedate as every other night, they readied themselves for bed. Having pulled his suspenders from his shoulders, grandfather peeled himself out of his incredibly long shirt. This antiquated clothing calmed me. In particular, the countless hooks on my grandmother's dusky rose underwear seemed very trustworthy and sound to me. That precisely such underwear, corsages with hooks and eyelets and stockings held up by garters, are now considered wicked, and that women wear them when going on a date, is emotionally quite beyond me.

For me, its code is completely different. That's my grandmother with her stockings buttoned on, and there's my Pippi Longstocking costume from primary school with the garter stockings and the legs in different colors. I found this salvation from tights absolutely perfect, and of course with no sexual connotations at all. The added benefit, that this kind of garment was many years later found attractive by third parties, was simply a collateral benefit I used. I still can't understand it. For me, these were the right clothes. I find it surprising that there is an overlap between practical and sexy. Layer upon layer of skirts and aprons then covered the underwear. “Housewives in pants”, as word at home had it, were those unsound folks from the city with whom one had no contact. The cousins – and to this extent I do feel that, as the preferred grandchild, I was seriously privileged – clearly had no idea how useful the taciturn nature of my grandparents was. Because anyone who talks little asks few questions. I found adults who constantly asked about how I was or other things physically repugnant. My grandparents were satisfied if I watched with a keen eye and helped but kept my peace on the verbal front; and conversely, they never seemed ridiculous: My grandmother never said she was going to make me a jam sandwich, and my grandfather most certainly never commented on peeling a pear. This communication structure was bereft of feeling shame for the other person and, more broadly speaking, low on irritation. From there, to put it bluntly, things went downhill. If I am now present in one of my own holes when someone there is doing the housework, then what would presumably otherwise occur in silence becomes a kind of radio football commentary, with every move on the pitch described. “I’m just taking a break and having a coffee; I’m going to water the flowers and then I’ll check the letterbox.” Oh, really. Stunning. Since, during this non-stop voice-over, I can’t do anything else, I could just as well do the work myself, and better because then it would be done the way I want. Why the soundtrack? Thomas Mann is said to have spent three hours a day writing in silence, and everyone in the house had to be quiet. I’d love to be that Thomas Mann – or hard of hearing. If someone addresses me when I am reading or writing, it definitely turns me into that other Thomas, Thomas Bernhard. Unjust and snorting like a bull. And I then cease to like myself. How good to have different places of work and to be able to withdraw. That in itself helps. That’s the architecture of happiness (Alain de Botton, THE ARCHITECTURE OF HAPPINESS, [New York, 2006]) and Virginia Woolf’s A ROOM OF ONE’S OWN. It’s

easy to prove my observation. On days when other, highly personal motives take the forefront for the service providers, my training, and later my household or my devotion to grandchildren or orderly schooling for my children, are no longer important: an appointment, training days, general meetings, holidays, the dog dies. So much for guaranteed support here and a service mindset there.
The phenomenon to be observed in kindergarten, school, and the household can regrettably not be transposed onto my work. With my work, there is no way of simply rearranging a few vases to be appealing or to leave the gravy boat extracted from the dishwasher on the top. You can't send out an author's copy of the text you last published casually. Even talking about writing is not casual enough. At best, someone then says: "With your ambition, you'll get there." That's not support but merely a variation on "Men are geniuses, women are diligent". How worrying and yet comforting, then, that other women who publish fare similarly. In her ON THE BENEFITS OF FRIENDSHIP, Isabelle Graw describes the phenomenon of marginalization of her own work by highlighting how a friend continuously bangs on about his own work, while her own publication does not garner a single comment. Demanding a conversation does not help. Anyone asking for such is inviting a war of destruction, she says. I read Sarah Cooper's HOW TO BE SUCCESSFUL WITHOUT HURTING MEN'S FEELINGS with a kind of pleasant dismay. There's still a place for diplomacy. And so I have adopted a mindset equivalent to the idea that "happy they who can say that they see another way".... Refining the diplomatic back and forth is not that good for training humility. But it is immensely efficient.

In some way or other, I must have known this while still in primary school because I already behaved accordingly back then. If I wanted to be accepted, then the motto had to be not in any way to let on that I had read most of the entire schoolbook already and was streets ahead of the rest of the class. Don't let them fall too far behind, that was clear.

Things always went well if I was so far ahead in the material we were learning if I got a good grade for contributing to class. Knowing too much is considered being a smart aleck. Being part of a cohort and yet standing out from it for one's knowledge is not smart; no, it is far worse, it is social suicide. Top grades typically don't go to the smart aleck, as you don't look like you've made an effort. That's crazy, and this view of the world leaves you very lonely. Instead of you bagging the best grade, the teacher invariably gives you only the second-best grade irrespective of how good you were, with the crazy and erroneous argument that this will spur you on. What to do in such an upside-down situation? Nurturing my innate joyful outlook proved to be a good means to counter this tough headwind. I got used to indulging in effusive optimism that let me feel like these early insights would pay off if only they could be properly metabolized. Faith moves mountains, or so the proverb would have it. For me, my campaign of transcendence, as it were, cut through the knots and blockades. It's like in medicine.

If it heals you it must be the right drug

If something functions well, I am not about to weigh myself down with unfruitful thoughts of why precisely that is. In religious education classes, in the course of spontaneous exuberance I explored the limits of the system of expectations. Many years before graduating from high school, we convent students were supposed to link our own leanings and skills with a possible profession. As if we had any idea of what the world outside was like. However, evidently even in good schools there are lessons devoted to pointless rambling. That said, I also suspected that with this inappropriately open issue the teachers wanted to sound us out in social terms. In boarding schools, one standard strategy is to woo the children of celebrities and similar sensational kids, and, on the other, to triumphantly enjoy the moment when the children of the bigwigs fail completely. Which is why I always answered the question of why I was at boarding school (after all, it was hardly because of my grades, which were, after all, excellent) by saying I was a problem child. What else could I have said? "Well, my parents are elitist and think boarding school is great?" Years later in acting classes, I had a colleague whose father, it transpired, was a gynecologist. "Why is your dad a gynecologist?", he was constantly being asked by brash young actors. I was immediately taken by his response: "He likes women." He knew how to do it. When asked what profession I imagined myself taking in the future I, at any rate, said "terrorist". People then laughed a lot. When I followed up by saying that my exaggerated sense of justice and my anger were great prerequisites in this regard, and that I didn't faint if I saw blood, listeners fell over backwards with laughter. The upshot was that I got selected to take part in the school's acting group. Up until that point, no one had taken the slightest bit of notice of the fact that outside school I had been professionally active in acting and cabaret. The religious education teacher, who prompted the acting group to take me on board, presumably had a possible therapeutic intent and considered acting less as a form of art. And once again I had learned something: Personal abysses, secrets, and highly unpleasant things should preferably be exaggerated when talking to others, so they always have the chance to think you're joking. That tactic gets you far, and not just in the art world. Incomprehensible? How often was I out and about with someone and people greeted us with suspicion. "This is XY, we live together," is as effective a stratagem as responding to "But that's not your husband!" by saying "Damn, I hadn't noticed. Why do I say 'darling' to everyone?" A good joke thrives on the next one following. Once everyone has laughed, you simply turn to the man and say: "And what was your name again?"

Everything embroidered on dishcloths is true

We can consider it a proven fact that one or other of the clichéd ideas on life my mother spouted is true. In school, what you learn is for life. Today, what was undesirable advance learning at school is an information edge as regards art. To put it bluntly: At an exhibition preview, you must not be too well informed, as otherwise you will disturb the conversational flow, which is driven by unanimity among those present. If you strongly state something that departs too far from the canon of suitable descriptions of art and art producers, then the others feel they are being shown up. So, forget those insightful interjections, and certainly don't preach: If everyone is of the opinion that XYZ is a feminist position, then let that one pass for today. Hey, feminism is not a matter of some static definition. So be generous and put it this way: Women who work seriously for money instead of sipping latte macchiato are feminists. The main problem to be solved, namely, how to avoid being a cynic, is all too obvious here. But how can one do so successfully?

Life goal: Don't become filled with bitterness

Evading cynicism is by no means a completely trivial matter. I view my education by the Franciscan nuns as a real advantage. For St. Francis, as their patron, spoke to birds and had a very interesting monetary system. This is possibly where I get the ability, when in doubt, to find something bizarre enough to laugh about rather than fall into abject despondency. And what standards do I adopt on the assets side of the sheet? The obverse of the observation of not being surrounded by excellence and superior insights is that you don't take the expert judgment of others seriously. If the judgments by the outside world are borne by considerations that have nothing to do with the matter at hand, then what standards should apply to one's own work? What counts as my yardstick in what is recognized to be a post-factual world? My highly personal solution is, I believe, to seize the bull by the horns. What I tend to do is expand my intrinsic abilities. I gladly accept outside affirmation, but it is not a precondition. To adapt and conform with mediocrity would itself be mediocre. This does not promote any education in humility. It's just you can't have everything, or so I say to myself and am overjoyed that I, too, can dish out the commonplaces left, right, and center. While keeping my eyes wide open to see who adopts a similar strategy. Sometimes I encounter the like-minded in unexpected places. Over dinner, the daughter of friends said quite innocently that the superb grades in German were a joke. A little bit of googling, no slavish copy-and-paste but a tweak to the sentence structure, and bingo, an "A". Completely undeserved, she continued. Just like her A Levels during her year in Britain. All of it nonsense. That was not, she claimed, the way to be prepared for the complex issues she would face at uni. Sounded pretty accurate to me, but, true to expectations, the company at table, chatting away gaily only a moment earlier, was irritated. What, the expensive year in Britain, nonsense? Serious parents who fear being downwardly mobile if the kids' grades are bad – now they dearly want a return on their investment in a girl's education. No one wants to hear that it's the same everywhere else. The daughter would have had a smoother ride of it if she'd said the level had been tough, but she was proud to have passed with good grades. How depressing.

Average in kind and quality

What counts here is what those opposite expect. The lawyers talk here of a performance that is average in kind and quality. How long did it take me to really grasp this? The knee-jerk response is to think of underperformance. However, my problem is my evidently undesired outperformance. If they are recognized as such on dating platforms, highly qualified women receive far fewer asks. The same post, without the academic references, would be greeted with far less silence. How to tolerate this if not with humor? How unjust! Over-qualified and thus possibly higher-earning women can safely avoid such portals and the membership fees and time they cost. I accordingly recommend my stipend-holders sign and seal the relationship they possibly want before graduation, as their chances will go downhill from there on in. Your defense against cynicism is tantamount to a muscle that requires regular training! In acting class, I learned how hard it is to speak like someone who thinks slowly and little. I was not very good at it. I was constantly scolded for talking too quickly and with too much modulation in my tone. Yet all I was doing was repeating a script and not uttering my own words. Nowadays, I devote a lot of energy to limiting myself to a few "bullets" and simplifying things. Small talk of average kind and quality is the objective. Conversations about art, however, as stated, do not really revolve around facts that could be the topic of discussion, as what is called for is knowledge appropriate to the situation. You convey that you are one of the initiated by namedropping and (very important!) by pronouncing names correctly. In this context, knowledge appropriate to the situation means that the pronunciation of a particular name may be specific to the group. Indeed, the pronunciation of the name can even be completely wrong, objectively speaking. In the case of some galleries, I even think that the hard-to-pronounce name, the hard-to-pigeonhole name, may be part of the reason for their success. People like the flavor of the name, and it thus stakes out your pitch. Or whatever. I find it calming each time the jury votes on the young person's word of the year. Elsewhere, this cultural technique has long been recognized and practiced.

Loops and Looped De Loop: Kindergarten is something for poor folk

Otherwise, I rely on the experiences I had back in my school days and give my insights greater depth: It is not about excellence in the loops of the reputation market that is the "Operating System Art" (see Jens Beckert, MARKETS FROM MEANING: QUALITY UNCERTAINTY AND THE INTERSUBJECTIVE CONSTRUCTION OF VALUE, Cambridge Journal of Economics, vol. 44, [2020], p. 285). The key thing the art market is about is elastic participation in the significance-creating communication loops of the art-market players. Socially adequate behavior is very challenging. You have to be constantly alert. That's what the opaqueness of the art market Is all about and is at the core of things: unwritten laws that you cannot file against and are forever being modulated by murky authority structures. FOMO, or the fear of missing out, is ostensibly in order here. Because you have to go with the flow. An early absence in my life made me aware of how knowledge arises in rhizomes. On my first few days at primary school, I was amazed by how familiar the other kids were with the system. I swiftly worked out why: They had all gone to kindergarten. My mother had razor-sharp words for such institutions. Although for once not in the form of a rhyme, but with true punch in terms of content, she countered my question of why I had not gone to kindergarten by pronouncing that a kindergarten is something for poor folk. Poor folk have to take jobs outside the home to earn money and therefore need someone to care for the kids. A battler slogan back then and today, which, having understood the one or other thing about elementary pedagogics since, I can relate to in various ways. The impact of the very different socialization and the attitude toward it was, at any rate, that I never ceased to be amazed. Like the Chinese man who ends up in Munich after time-traveling (Herbert Rosendorfer, LETTER BACK TO ANCIENT CHINA, [Huntingdon, 2003), I was very surprised by the rites widespread among the children. Since much was worked out verbally (I wasn't yet able to read back then anyway), my enquiries tended to be at least funny. Art forms such as Lothar Baumgarten's oeuvre, with his anthropological considerations, were to appear completely and utterly logical to me at a much later point in life.

There are nc semi-albinos

The consternation at primary school remained entrenched on both sides, or rather on three sides, as the teaching staff and the pupils each formed a referential system of their own. Straw-blond and almost translucently white-skinned, I stood before these creatures not knowing what to do. What had they ostensibly been taught in that kindergarten? Common domestic sense it had not been. I heard the adults talking about me, thinking I was out of earshot, saying that a structured preschool was a must if I was to be able to catch up at all. They looked at me with concern. Evidently, I was semi-albino, they assumed. "There are no semi-albinos," I thought to myself. I felt like I was in Communist East Germany. My plan was to overtake them rather than catch up, because what they wanted me to catch up on through "structured learning" seemed pretty useless to me.

I certainly didn't want to become like them. At any rate, I found the others to be astonishingly uneducated, given that they had already spent a seeming lifetime in preschool. Why did they know nothing? My light skin tone was, in their eyes, sick, whereas for me it was normal. There were no signs of an illness. Essentially, I had never been sent to a doctor. I was even born at home. There were serious reservations against "maternity advice", as my mother called it. My mother talked about the people who worked in the field as if she were describing a secret service. We certainly had not let them spy on us. How smart of her. Decades later, I spent some time researching the continuity in education from the Nazi doctrines through to present-day Germany. So much for the notion that any child can fall asleep! So much for not raising domestic tyrants. It was all about raising soldiers bereft of empathy (Sigrid Chamberlain, ADOLF HITLER, DIE DEUTSCHE MUTTER UND IHR ERSTES KIND: ÜBER ZWEI NS-ERZIEHUNGSBÜCHER, [Adolf Hitler, German mothers and their first child: On two Nazi books on education, Giessen, 2010]) Just as they thought I was some abnormal curiosity; I invariably assumed my classmates were not very gifted. How could you offer a rat in the schoolyard your break-bun? Small wonder that a seemingly trustworthy rat then bit you and you immediately had to be vaccinated and everyone then spent the next few days waiting to see whether you would die or, as my fellow pupils seemed to assume was also possible, might turn into a wolf. Why a wolf of all things, why not into a rat? How could you hang up your jacket on a peg next to all the other jackets and be surprised if you caught lice? Why paint a "horse as faithfully as possible" if there were some standing around outside that you could touch? If you painted a horse then you painted a really special one, say in blue. My mother warned me. Keep your cards to yourself. Now and again, however, I let an unfiltered thought slip out, and I commented with such clumsiness on my art teacher. The woman was as big as I was. On her, her handbag looked like a suitcase. Everything is, after all, a question of ratios. I wondered whether she wore children's shoes and whether the “Liliputians” whom I had seen in a theme park (that’s what they were called there) lived in a caravan with tiny furniture. Maybe the amusing little people in the theme park were her relatives. I would no doubt get slightly darker hair on growing up and no longer be flaxen blond like my grandmother. She entrusted her ash-blond hair to a fine mesh that looked like a spider’s web.

Angela Glajcar SASA
Photo: Jürgen T. Sturany → 103

On special holidays, my hair was also tied in a bit of a bun on the top of my head and placed in such a net, making it look a bit like a donut. The idea that you could have one and the same hairstyle for over eight decades was calming. What in art is an artist’s unmistakable style was also something that existed for people’s everyday lives, too. The vocab for this (style, uniform, etc.), or what my children would now term “iconic”, I simply didn’t have; but without technical terms for it, the canon of unwavering standards gradually grew: no tights, little variance in hairstyle, and finally, no trousers. A strategic combination of USP, unmistakability, and little effort. At the time when I had the clumsy conversation, my hair was as bright as what my grandmother called “angel’s hair” and draped over the branches of the Christmas tree. I generally found it an advantage to have angel’s hair. Angels later became elves, I knew. And angels are always good.

Elves are al manner of things

Many of these (in part highly debatable) deductions buzzed around my head, and the tiny teacher seemed far more of a curio to me than I was. In my eyes, she was an old child. Somehow petulant and with as little knowledge of her subject as the idiots who had almost caught rabies. Standing around in the schoolyard seemed pretty out of place to my mind anyway. Why, for God’s sake? I found it embarrassing that we could be seen from the street. We must look like prisoners. The old child with the turquoise lids painted over her eyes criticized the thick meaty tail of the horse I had painted, and suddenly I found myself saying: “If you want a picture with a real horse on it, then simply photograph one.” Complications followed.

Who cares about milk when you’ve cut your teeth?

The children who surrounded me at primary school watched children’s movies in which people drank milk straight from a cow. But everybody knows it can be poisonous, I thought. Decades later, I read in a newspaper that children had died because their mothers had drunk unpasteurized milk. Then there was a time when drinking cow’s milk was completely out. Today, animal milk is only slightly better than smoking. Ersatz products that derive from plants are importantly called milk. Soybean milk. Oat milk. What sort of a milk cult has popped up? As a preschool child, I was sent off with a metal can to get the milk. The milk then disappeared into puddings and cakes, but certainly never got drunk. In fact, milk was largely irrelevant. For me, milk was sustenance for the calves and for the crazy city dwellers. Who cares about milk when you’ve cut your teeth? That’s more or less how I saw it as a farm child. I watched people on TV drinking milk. In those happy family series, there was a glass of milk next to each child’s plate, and they then promptly grew milky moustaches. Meaning they weren’t even able to drink properly. If you know how to drink, you don’t end up with the beverage on your face. On holiday in Bavaria, I watched men who wiped off the bath foam that sat thick on the top of their drinks off their faces with crumpled handkerchiefs and looked around heartily. The bath foam in the tub at home didn't taste of anything. I didn't dare ask anyone what all of this meant. At school, at any rate, you were expected to part with small coins for school milk. My mother didn't give me any money for school milk. They're mad, she ordained. Since we were not often of the same opinion, I very much appreciated this merging of minds on the topic of school milk. At the same time, I came under pressure, as I did not know how to put my mother's instruction to keep my cards close to my chest into practice at school. If you're the only person who does not put your school-milk money on the table, what will the others think of you? That you're forgetful or poor? I found it completely inexplicable why teachers then said, surely, since I came from a farm, I knew how good milk was for you. Quite the opposite was the case! Since, in my view, I came from well-informed circles, I sided with my mother's opinion that they were all quite mad. My mistrust of all things relating to nutritional advice thus rests on deep-seated foundations laid at an early stage in life. For me, it was clear as crystal glass that something which was stored in little packets and could hang around for months without being refrigerated, only to be distributed by a janitor who had a half-empty cigarette packet boasting a dromedary in his blue apron pocket, could not be healthy and right, but unsound. I believed that specifically my rejection of the variants "vanilla" and "strawberry" spoke considerably in my favor. How were strawberries supposed to have got into such small packets? Why did "natural" and the version with the vanilla aroma cost the same? I sensed some poorly concealed fraud. I was unable to convince others of my assessment of the state of things. I quite simply did not have the right words to do so and had to endure the fact that the others thought me deranged or that my family was poor. I felt it considerably worse to be thought of as forgetful. No way could I persuade anyone at home with statements such as "all the others do it". If I wanted something from my parents, I needed to justify my needs solely in terms of myself and the benefits to the household. An automobile because everyone got one – no traction. The wish for my own car in order to run errands, to be flexible, to not have to rely on being given a ride by "dubious chivalrous men", as my dad liked to call them – now that got fulfilled. At any rate, as regards school milk, I thought: "It's dirt, but there's nothing I can do about it." It was obvious to me that there was nothing I knew to say to the teachers and the other kids that would sound so educated and superior as those sententious words the mayor declaimed when addressing my grandparents on their birthdays. The vicar visited my grandmother only on such occasions. No one offered me a reason why. I decided to take note of this question until I was able to find an answer to it. A good memory and patience are a combination that I found to be as good as bread fresh from the oven with ice-cold butter on it. Pure enjoyment, and something that tasted good till the cows came home. Now that saying with the butter was something I, in turn, found so good that I imagined perhaps I could myself become mayor at some point. I immediately discarded the thought. I wanted either to live my life on a solitary farmyard like the one I knew from birth, or in a completely different way, namely slap bang in the middle of a big city. A small town was out of the question. For me, that would be the sum of all things bad from both worlds. You would have no peace and quiet, and you'd have a view into the distance, but also neighbors. Neighbors always look out of their windows and have an opinion on everything – opinions that were no doubt pretty much of the same quality as my teachers' thoughts on painted horse tails and school milk. And in a small town, you don't have a glorious theater or the other similar stuff you have in big cities. In a big city, you ride by streetcar and get out whenever you want. You never have to hunt for a parking space, and you don't go shopping in stores that have a huge parking lot in front of them. I would wear dresses and long coats and stay standing during the short trip by tram. Because that's when the beautiful dresses look their elegant best. Practical anoraks you wore when driving by car would not exist in my world – no one would have them. The children in the small town seemed to me to be waiting for something. At any rate, they spent a lot of time sitting around at bus stops. As if life came by a bus stop. For my part, I was out in the fields and woods. I didn't wait for anything, but observed the work the adults did or compared the illustrations in my book of plants with what I saw on my wanderings. I loved the scent of clover when the sun shone on it, and the feeling of almost slipping up between the plants on a wet field of beet. The children from the nearest village, by contrast, were busy deciphering words scrawled on the bus stops and watching cars go by. They seemed tired to me. In big cities, and I knew both Vienna and Frankfurt, the children chatted away with their parents. They seemed lively and were well-dressed. That was what I wanted. What seemed like a century later, I sat with my godchild in the streetcar in Düsseldorf, talking about this and that, when I heard someone say: "They're Jews. They talk a lot with children." A very opaque situation. For all my eloquence and the studies I have made since the thing with the school milk, I repeatedly find myself in situations where I think "That is so wrong that I don't know what to do". Correcting it is problematic, and where to start? Sometimes in comparable moments without a line of address or a closing line I write in mails:

I find the whole thrust distastefu

On bad days, I send the email off. Bad days are rare. And becoming even rarer. Better than mails, meaning contact with the outside, is contact with the inside. Idem: keeping a diary. See above. Since barking at people doesn't help or, as the communications specialist would say, you need to bring someone on board but there is no one to onboard who understands even the welcome on board, the best form is to converse with yourself – in a diary. Another motto from the calendar or dishcloth: Talking to yourself is a guarantee of a lifelong, cultured conversation. Keeping a diary is even better, as actually talking to yourself can irritate. When I was in primary school, I had no real safety valve. Talking to myself dreamily came to me naturally. In children, that's not being disturbed, but normal. Everything is a matter of the referential system, I say, repeating myself. Today, I'm at Volume 91 of my diary. Diary attempts during my first few years at boarding school were abandoned, as I had no interest in having to discuss the content of my diary with my mother. Personal privacy, the inviolability of mail, discretion as regards third-party rights, none of that played a role in my mother's life. Her relationship to ownership protocols also had its gaps. Rebelling against her was pointless. I found getting through a school day tricky enough without waging battle on the home front, too. Instead, I trained my memory. The result of my mother's invasive nature was that I essentially had no intimately private sphere that she could violate. Added to which, little is the space around me that can be touched without injury. I can keep my distance all the same. In this regard, I am a bit of a curiosity myself. For from everything I hear, this was not to be expected. I like my pragmatism. I thought it was only a question of time. I would be leading most of my life without her commentaries and would be able to write whatever I liked, wear whatever I liked. Thanks to boarding school, I was able to largely withdraw from her grasp early on in life.

To paint s not to draw

I treat the positive effects of a negative socialization without bitterness or a sense of triumph. I treat the positive results of negative attempts at schooling the same way. My primary schooling was remarkably poor on balance. I learned from it that you have to keep your eyes open and scout around outside school for what can be useful and be mistrustful of what is placed before you. After all, possibly it's all wrong and won't stand up to critical inspection. The schoolbook said you should paint something, but it was all about drawing something. Comical place where you can't even distinguish painting from drawing. Or so I thought, and I considered that in that precise moment the word "comical" was spot on and much better than "strange". It was enough to make me laugh and not just absurd. My mother, of course, also had a motto at hand, albeit one that was not always unconditionally useful: "If your teacher says water flows up the hill, then say: It's already up there." Confusing and crazy. So I kept my cards close to my chest, not just on the issue of school milk but also on the content of lessons that did not seem very sound, and perfected sidestepping and terrain-shifting techniques. No interest in gym? You don't say no to something shared; no, you say yes to something socially recognized. A visit to the theater, for instance. Or you needed to read something. Or knit something. But definitely never a no. All of which initially happened in the hope that once I was at long last an adult, things would be more sensible and freer. As a child, I thought adults were able to say no to all manner of things. I thought wrong.

Jonathan Meese ARCHAEOPTERYX
Doll: Markus Spatzier → 103

No is not socially acceptable

A sub-complex approach to the world leads, in general, to only a "yes" being perceived positively. Here, a "that's not necessarily true" fits perfectly. No one would say that a "yes-man" has positive connotations. Back then, in girls' school, I had a role in Bertolt Brecht's opera for the school, THE YES-MAN AND THE NO-MAN. The teacher who rehearsed the parts with us mentioned in passing that Brecht had admittedly chosen the sharp term "Yes-Man" for publication, but one could definitely ask what woman was behind the idea. This sentence truly buzzed around my head. My skepticism throughout life towards ostensible geniuses has its roots in that sentence. Nevertheless. In daily life, a "no" is simply not well received. Not that I have anything against a good old "yes". For example, if someone offers me a glass of alcohol or offers to marry me. But when it comes to art, I am evidently a bit of a mule. Experience shows: "No" is not a good word in the art market. If I say no to an offer to buy, then the "no" is not accepted. Is it still the case that a no from a woman is treated like a semi-coquettish "yes"? Preferably not. And it would seem not to be the case. A high-speed survey in my own part of the art world revealed, with no votes against: Men fare exactly the same. I try to avoid a direct no and sidestep it with a "That's not my issue." Or: "That's not my conflict." Which is why I don't want to buy it. It has nothing to do with me, and I collect art because the collection is supposed to have something to do with me. I have little success with this. Why can't I just say I gladly attend previews if I am interested in the artist? I appreciate even the most expensive of dinners only if I am seriously considering buying a piece. Objectively speaking, that is considerate of me, or so I imagine, as I spare the gallery's resources. At the same time, those who stand with their backs to the art and are only there for the wine and company are equally unwelcome. Or not? Probably the truth lies somewhere in-between. A few people need to be present at any art occasion in order to give rise to that specific gallery atmosphere, and those who can afford art but at this very moment are simply there for the wine – now they can be won over.... Because gallerists who have 30 different items in their portfolio can persuade even those who are so well informed? Of course, they can. At any rate, it is constantly being attempted with the right shot of self-confidence. I always find it very odd when someone who does not know me whatsoever tries to educate me. Do other people feel the same? Definitely, or so I think, because I have set out to no longer feel insulted.

Authoritarian invitations

The following has happened to me not once, but repeatedly over time. Having on several occasions attempted to be struck off a mailing list by sending an email or a postcard, I now call up and say: "Please take me off your mailing list." And astonishingly: People do not desist from sending invitations because they feel sure I will rave about the one or other item if only I first see it. They do not want to miss the opportunity to acquaint me… Is there anybody out there who really believes this? Do these people listen to their own voices? Let's take it step by step: A recipient of invitations to commercial exhibitions says: "I do not want to receive these invitations." The sender replies, no, I will not stop sending them because I must have an opportunity to convince you. How's that supposed to work? It's actually illegal. Sure, the art market is no great friend of data privacy laws. Because data privacy regulations also reflect the excesses of bad behavior and megalomania. Oh well. You can, after all, simply throw away mail without opening it. In the case of direct personal contact, by contrast, you need to have your wits about you. Irrespective of how experienced and skillful I may now think I am, there are on occasion new variations of paternalistically grabbing hold of you and invading your personal space that catch me completely by surprise and at times actually rip the rug from under my feet: The invitation to have dinner on a weekday seemed a no-brainer. It was extended by people with whom I had, on occasion, had areas of professional and private contact. We knew each other a bit better than just from afar. The evening initially proceeded in the expected friendly-cum-preachy chatty tone. However, during the main course I was offered a partnership in a gallery that the hosts declared they were oh-so-happy to be able to broker. Hang on, to be precise, it was not even offered to me, but my husband was asked whether he could not fulfill my wish in this regard. That was so radically unheard-of and wrong on so many levels that I at first thought I was hearing a joke. As not only had I thought I'd been doing something by way of a career that fitted me like a glove and had earned my keep for decades and inwardly experienced this as real satisfaction, but I had also expected that the outside world could readily see how the vocation so suited me. Well, that was clearly wrong. Because on the other side of the table, there was a semi-conspiratorial huddle claiming I had always wished for this. So how was I to contradict? I should simply have said "No" thrice. No, I had not wished for that. No, money is not the only path to a gallery, and had I wanted one I would have set one up myself and would not seek to take a stake in one that already existed. That would have all been far too intimate. And aggressive. Not that I could get a word in edgeways. Some patterns are forever being repeated.

Work should not be conflated with fun

I didn't have to wait long to hear the next statement on the other side of the table. Having a gallery would be a lot of fun for me! Things were going downhill fast: fun?! The dysfunctional conversation thus now included another really bad level. Evidently those present had different ideas of what function work is supposed to have in life. Because I, for one, carefully avoid the term "fun" when talking about a money-earning profession. Fun is something I associate with private activities. For me, fun has something exuberant about it. The idea that work should be fun across the entire duration of your working life seems unrealistic to me and is therefore most definitely a one-way street to dissatisfaction.

A few decades' worth of scribbling paper

I encounter the constellation every few years when decisions have to be made on my children's schooling and/or when I am confronted with such decisions in other households: The legally incompetent are expected to decide what school they want to go to, what instrument they "like" playing, and whether they would "enjoy" a gap year abroad. The change in social circle, learning, ties severed, and efforts across longer periods of time – are these things that should be linked to such hedonistic motives? Heaping inappropriate responsibility on the shoulders of legal minors? It's a constellation where, to my mind, so much is so wrong. Even kindergartens now seem to have corporate identities. Everything is especially special (see, of course: Reckwitz, A SOCIETY OF SINGULARITIES). I do believe my expectation that I would learn to read, write, and do arithmetic in primary school and would need to devote a few hours a day to this was far too narrow and yet too broad a hope. Today, children are constantly occupied doing something; they have days that are filled to bursting and no genuinely free weekends, and instead draining homework to do and projects to prepare. Parents likewise always have something to do and talk the cake spread to death while endlessly discussing the right, healthy school food and water in glass bottles. Seventeen mothers and one father who are busy at handicrafts are addressed as "craftswomen" in the round-robin email. Evidently, even in the course of a few years at school, you don't necessarily learn the basics of joint productive learning, such as sticking to the appropriate noise level or to stand two-by-two in a row without complaining if it makes things easier. In terms of content,

I continue to find a lot of things strange. That said, the good thing about primary school pupils is that when they move on to other schools, there is a real surfeit, one that will last for years, of paper to scribble on. Exercise books in which only two pages have been used. I have since then stockpiled writing and craft materials – in a really big way. The lists of mandatory materials at the beginning of each school year were detailed down to the hardness of three different pencils and the number of hairs on various paintbrushes. Learning to grasp what you read, and to reproduce excerpts of it, to write a letter, or to calculate increases in prices – now that seems to be something you're supposed to learn at home. There is no space in the middle of all those circles of school chairs for spelling. It's quite in order that I have to teach my children a lot of things myself. Because I have benefited immensely from their time in primary school. Much of it can be transposed onto my profession and how I approach art. Should not every collection have its very own profile? Who dares actually say: I collect examples of the zeitgeist. My collection is a child of the times in which we live. Or: I buy art the way others buy a car. Once it was a Beetle, now it's a Tesla. Simply the things you buy. School parties with muffins and exhibition previews with fried miniatures likewise have a lot in common. This is true specifically as regards the depth of conversations at the event itself and the lack of focus and efficiency in the preparation of the events. How many mails go flying back and forth about a loan for an exhibition before it is finally clear what the collector's name is and whether they do in fact want to be mentioned using that moniker in the catalog. Once things have finally been settled, sometimes even after the date on which the exhibition formally opens, I get three invitations to the preview, each with a different variant of my name, and the work is then presented in the catalog the wrong way round. How many preliminary discussions have been held, how many piles of materials sifted, how many tons of materials have been used for an exhibition, and then, during the private view in praise of the artist, in her address the director of the museum consistently mispronounces the artist's name? Time would appear not to be a scalable factor in the "school" or "art" worlds. Because if the time came at a price, then it would be cheaper to simply buy everything for the cake spread than to be forever coordinating who will bake what cake and bring it along. Possibly, in some cases it would even be cheaper to give museums an acquisitions budget rather than financing some inefficient round of loans. Years ago, a piece insured at 2,000 Euros was borrowed from a museum, and a different piece, one that did not in the least resemble the first, was sent back after the end of the exhibition. The curator at some point proposed I simply arrange to swap it back with the other collector myself. There should be a dictionary of art-market and school terms that are not synonyms: Diligent is not productive. Active is not effective. Well-meant does not imply well made.

Space for your own pairs of terms:

What exactly do I do professionally, alongside the above-mentioned studio management, that is so hard to convey? Abstractly speaking, I am formally recognized as a self-employed person (lawyer) specialized (in line with my interests and gifts) in art. Potentially, my studies (law) and my career (court-appointed expert) are suited to consistently generating an income. As stated, my approach to my professional activity seems, to my mind, intrinsically logical, whereas on the outside it may seem somewhat bloodless. Thankfully, I am self-employed and do not have to apply for jobs. Because in an HR department where people expect you to be gunning for the job, I would not stand a chance with my unexciting track record: In my role as a court-appointed expert for contemporary art, as a lawyer specialized in the daily business and strategic thrust of artistic studios and collections, the object of my work is socially mainstream, interesting, and luxurious. By socially mainstream, I mean that my professional titles are decidedly class-specific, and since I predominantly interact with my own social class, there is rarely profound annoyance. Only on occasion do I come into contact with criminal offenders in the fields of forgery and the sale of stolen goods. Slightly more frequently, I am involved in cases of defrauding insurance companies (usually only attempts to do so). Money laundering crimes are a topic treated academically and satirically in my law office (see, for example, my column in the legal journal GELDWÄSCHE UND RECHT [Money Laundering & the Law] published by Deutscher Fachverlag, satirizing how money laundering might function in the art market). I find the work interesting because it means I am close to art and the people associated with it. My passion is art, and in my job, I can experience the production processes and the discourse close up, at times even from the inside perspective. I consider it a luxury in my job that I can exclusively concern myself with art. Because this means for me that I live in a safe and secure community. If there are plenty of resources for art, then things around it can’t be all bad. I have always kept my distance from conflictual, highly serious fields of law, such as family law. Since I had the opportunity to stake my claim in an exotic discipline, I seized it, gladly and deliberately. And this also served to tack past various potential unpleasantries, such as hierarchies and rigid job models. That the work has now functioned smoothly for decades is, however, as I now know, the result of the fact that I have a good memory and that the core element of my talent is satire. I am accordingly well entertained most of the time. Added to which, my wage-earning occupation is structured such that the tasks can be handled productively and without a racing heart. Things are, above all, managed in such a way that they don't cost me sleep or stomach cramps. It's all so completely unsensational. My favorite idea of work is to be "silently chirpy" while active. Now that may sound quirky, but today I think that "silently chirpy" is nothing other than an old-fashioned description of what is now faddishly termed a good work-life balance. Or to be even more accurate, a good "work-life blending", because life and work blend if you busy yourself with something professionally that aligns with your private interests, and the social circle in which you move in your profession largely coincides with that in your private life. An island life.

Gabriele Stötzer
TRANS VOR- UND ZURÜCKDREHEND
(TRANS TURNING FORWARD AND BACKWARD)

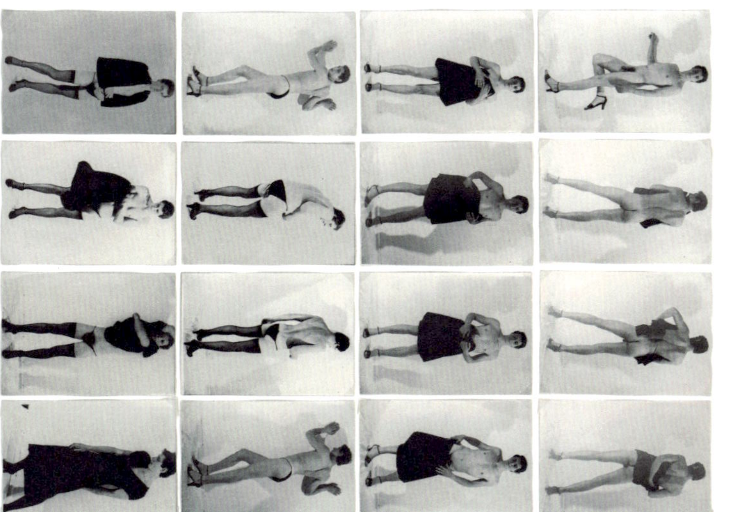

Jenny Holzer PROTECT ME FROM WHAT I WANT
Olaf Holzapfel (hay object), Angela Glajcar

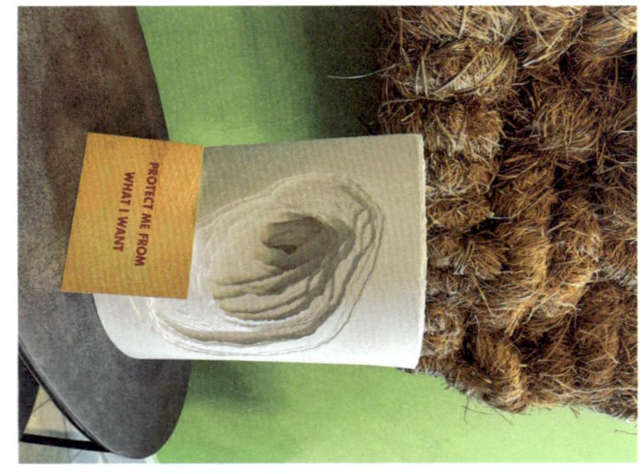

Elisabeth von Samsonow A FAIRY
IN THE EARTH'S GRAVITATIONAL
FIELD, Diaries

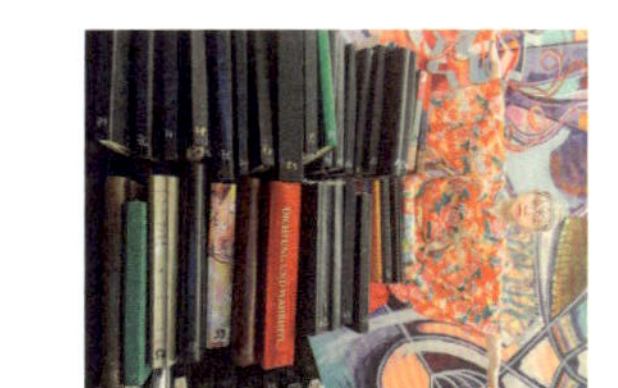

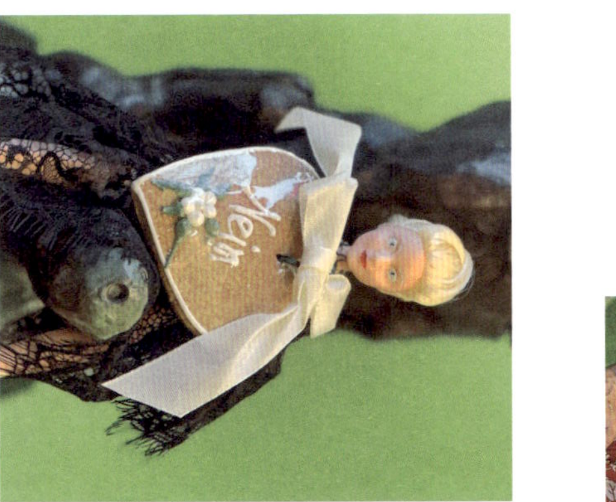

Jonathan Meese ARCHAEOPTERYX
Doll: Markus Spatzier

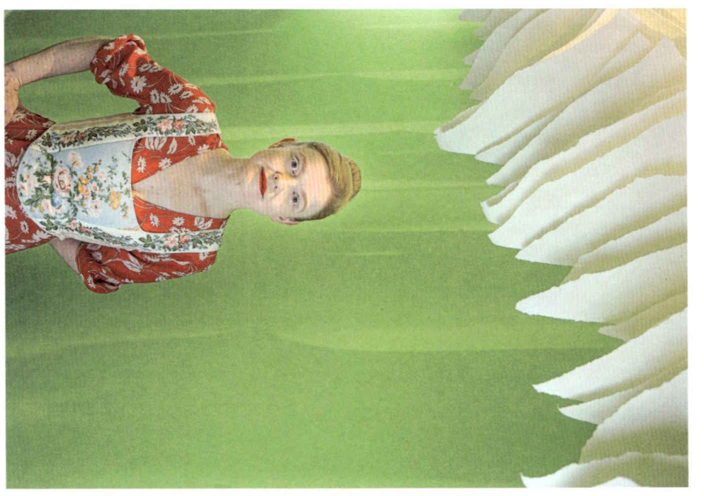

Angela Glajcar SASA
Photo: Jürgen T. Sturany

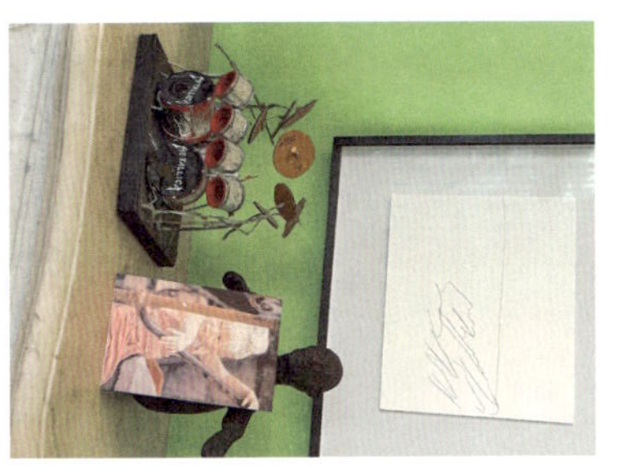

Rose Eken DRUMKIT, Stephan Balkenhol
HUMPTY DUMPTY, Bettina Blohm CORNWALL,
Sasa four years old

The private museum – tribunal in your own rooms

A collector and client once criticized the way I have structured my life: "You've once again made it too easy for yourself." I self-confidently countered the charge: "No idea why I should make it too hard for myself." Down through the years, this became a standard couplet when we met. A little while ago, in a high-end stationary store, various articles suddenly bore the sentence, dripping in significance and wrongly attributed to Goethe: Collectors are happy people. What twaddle. I immediately heard my father objecting, and it's obvious what he would have said: "Only true to a limited extent." In my then perception, collectors, regardless of how effusive and self-certain they were, were also driven by something that leaves your soul all furrowed. This peripheral knowledge did not trigger any consequences. And why should it have done? It all had nothing to do with me. However, let's go back in time a bit. Something has changed since then. Interweaving it with a professional context, an acquaintance sent me to the almost complete private museum of widowed collector Klaus F. K. Schmidt. There he stood before me, a somewhat shy man. His approach to art was, at first sight, the usual mixture of unstructured, sentimental, fiery, and juvenilely in-your-face. In conversation with him, I was offered the well-known disconnected detailed knowledge. As always. However, there was something beneath it all that was new to me and immediately captured my attention. In the approach to art, I sensed an unprotected yearning, and I really pricked up my ears when I discovered a form of productive originality: a collector who only buys through galleries. Now that I'd never heard of. In my lectures, I always joke about collectors who purchase in studios. In a witty vein, I then describe how collectors usually proceed. Buying from an artist in the studio is a bit like going to a concert. In front of the stage are 120,000 fans, and on the stage, depending on my audience, I am Robbie Williams, Harry Styles, or Taylor Swift singing only for "you". If an artist distributes business cards at an exhibition and invites people to drop by the studio, then it's a bit like dealing with con artists, to my mind. The persons thus addressed feel themselves special and sense the advantage of being able to buy art without involving the gallery and thus at preferential conditions. They soon sober up when they find out that the artist's flaunting of the market rules leads to the prices for the works collapsing and the career curve flattening equally fast. And it's particularly unpleasant if, after decades, there is also no certificate of authenticity for the piece, if only because the gallery says drily: "Never seen that piece before in my life." Which is usually not even incorrect. A gallery may not be obliged to uphold the material truth of who originated the work. If something did not go down the official avenues, then precisely this certificate of authenticity is often lacking. Artists consciously do not remember things that were sold bypassing the gallery and often for cash. The fear of "the tax office" regularly plays a key role in this regard.

The collector blues

It was an incredible experience for me to meet someone who had employed no trickery in assembling a collection. I was delighted for once not to have a copycat collector before me. It was thus to a certain extent only logical that a private bond arose. You don't simply let someone like that disappear out of your life! However surprisingly accurate his opinions on art were, and close to my own, and however productive the interaction with the man was, everything that following was hard to weigh up and destabilizing. The meeting marked the provisional end of my life in the comfort zone. There was now an acute need to focus more closely on the phenomenon of "collector blues". Because my husband also had collector blues. I had not anticipated that I, too, could be affected by the collector's dissatisfaction. Collectors, with their approaches to life, had until then been phenomena in a different referential system. Retrospectively, I saw myself almost with defiance as exclusively an art market pro. The sphere of collectors had until then always overlapped here and there with my own path through life. But it all essentially took part very much on the peripheries of my professional work or, to be more precise, my perception. The elegant, high-end consumption of art increasingly took place without my being present. As a young woman, I had at least staffed a trade-fair booth or a gallery. Through my work in studio management and as a judicial expert, I had, over the years, drifted ever further away from the actually places where art changed hands. Because when collectors appear, my work has either already been done or has to be done afterwards. The exhibition has been initiated, the participation in the trade fair arranged, the contracts signed and sealed; bequeathals to descendants or a foundation don't happen till some later point in time. It is galleries and museums, and at times artists, who have the direct contact with collectors. As regards preparing expert opinions, the jobs tend to be commissioned by lawyer colleagues, by heirs, or the curators employed by collections, or even sometimes by the courts. Direct contact through a commission in person or a collector as the host of the evening dinner – now that was becoming an ever more infrequent occurrence. The contact was usually friendly, but always at arm's length. The price for the exotic field I had chosen, for occupying a small market niche, is the absence of any assumption that one had something in common. In art there are stereotype professions. The roles are firmly assigned, as emblematic as in a puppet theater. Punch, the policeman, Judy, the crocodile, etc. They are all there.

It is difficult to establish a new character alongside them all. The role of head of studio is largely unknown. If I explain that I am in charge of the strategic thrust – meaning, for example, the choice of gallery and the legal and commercial affairs of the artist generally – then this is not readily digested. At the end of the day, the person sitting opposite me or next to me at table thinks I am a gallerist or

Markus Spatzier, SASA AND ENGELBERT → 134

work in a studio as an assistant. The associations bound up with the task invariably and astonishingly miss the point and are, moreover, primarily connoted negatively. To stick with the image of the puppet theater: My role is located somewhere between Judy and the croc, and people then attempt to avoid me as if I were some annoying governess. I don't take this personally. After all, it is easy to grasp that only direct contact with the artist is quotable and therefore precious. No one wants to get stuck in an overfull waiting room. It can even be an advantage not to have a clear job designation from the list of self-employed occupations as regards your actual professional activities. Whenever someone asks, it is your free choice how you describe your work, inventing a new social tag or at least changing the usual emphasis. At times, I simply select one aspect of my work and reduce it radically to something like: "I'm the editor of the Angela Glajcar catalogue raisonné." Only rarely do I then face a follow-up question. At most along the lines of: "Huh, but she's still alive. Why do you need a catalog raisonné?" I like such a launchpad. Depending on my mood, I can then outline the importance of a well-researched catalog raisonné for the way the works' value develops and in general for an artist's career. I might equally well decide the situation calls for questions from me that sow confusion, such as an "Oh really?" The most frequent response if I refer to the catalog raisonné, which we update whenever a new work comes out, is that I am paternalistically taken to one side or openly mocked with an "Aren't you worried about the tax authorities?"

Taxes as a leitmotif

In Switzerland, the saying goes that whoever pays a lot of tax is in a good place, as high taxes mean you have a high income. So, concentrate on earning money. Taxes function as an indicator of success. In Germany, by contrast, tax avoidance is considered something you can brag about – preferably when you've been tricky and smart. Whether something is taxed and how it is taxed is not some natural law but rests on what is, at times, a somewhat arbitrary decision by the legislature. The widespread view among prospective heirs that the existing wealth essentially already belongs to them, and that the estate should be handled in their interest, overlooks the fact that the transition from one generation to the next is dealt with very differently from one country to the next and from one era to the next. Anyone who finds it unjust if the eldest son is considered the heir should remember that there is also a method whereby the youngest son gets it all. The thinking: The latter is of course younger and can hold office longer once the head of the family dies. The side-effect of uncertainty, namely that possibly another heir may be born, may potentially impact beneficially on the development of the descendants' personalities.

Dying creates heirs

Along the way to graduation and taking your bar exams, as a law student you have to learn a lot by heart. Just as I still hear my driving instructor speaking to me if I am to be able to park the car in one go, so I have countless mnemonic aids still in my head. Inheriting sounds positive for most people, but first of all someone has to have died. The legal mentor drummed it into me that dying creates heirs. That way, you always bear in mind that inheritance is, from the outset, potentially a troubled matter. Gifting owing to death sounds a bit better. However, testators often tussle with their own mortality and even more with the fact that they are not entirely free in their gifting decisions. Testators do not like the mandatory reserved portions of an estate. At the main forks in the road of life, people simply regress and want to act like they did at kindergarten age and "determine" everything. In one of the first lectures that I attended as a law student, I heard

that the German constitution was like dishwater that had
already been slightly used. Such water is never really clean,
but you can achieve amazing results with it. Transposed
onto inheritances, the dishwater with which you can get
quite a long way is to remember very simple legal principles; for example, the life goals of "not being open to blackmail" and "not having a bad conscience". You need not fear
siblings and divorced spouses if you took down a few pictures in your dead aunt's place before your co-heirs arrived
and sold this and that from the collection in your initial
joy at having at long last inherited something. Naturally
such things occur well before the precise assessment of how
the tax-exempt inheritance of art can actually occur in the
world of applicable law. I'm very happy in such settings
that I nurtured all those discussions I had with the staff at
the kindergarten on how my children were developing. I
didn't find out anything new about my children there, but I
decisively expanded my vocabulary to include insights such
as: At four, you can understand and apply many laws, albeit 1
depending on your abilities, only to third parties and not to
yourself. At five, it is not favorable if you are still modeling
matters such that your own behavior, which, objectively
speaking, violates the law, appears justified. At any rate, the
law of inheritance is a field that not only vividly shows how
arbitrarily prosperity is distributed and redistributed, but
also how greed functions.

Anyone who thinks greed is a positive feeling believes that porn is about love

What astonishes me is to see how people treat the legal framework. They evidently try to trick the chance corsetry of regulations in which we are all anchored whether we like it or not. Elaborate and at times even expensive contortions, to the point of taking up residence abroad and
.1 buying musical theaters in cities that you only know from the name on an interstate exit, are undertaken, all in the hope of reducing the tax load or another person's inheritance. In very many cases, that goal is not achieved. Such knowledge should be used circumspectly. It's not a good idea to try and stand in the way of the popular sport of "tax dodging". Otherwise bland folk suddenly blossom when enthusing about their purportedly exclusive knowledge of tricks to dodge tax. And they certainly don't want to hear anything to the contrary. In a sense, I actually understand that, as I also don't like being told how everything relating to tax and art functions. The marginal difference is that I concern myself with these topics by way of my profession and have even published the one or other article on them, but that is of no importance. I am forever stuck on the horns of a dilemma: Do I voice my expert views or instead prefer to avoid the risk of marginalization? ("Is what the young lady is saying really true?"). As a result, I may not be successful. Because if someone listens to me, I have also provided legal counsel free of charge. Which would also

not be professional behavior. Meaning taxes and art are not good material for small talk. I prefer to be treated as not completely on the ball and therefore hold my tongue. I let the abstract opportunity that my real expertise in these matters might shine through and I could woo future clients pass. What helps the maneuver is that in the art context it is predominantly drinks that are provided. And drinks function in communication like a fan did in the hand of a woman in ancient times. The social function of drinks at exhibition openings is, in my opinion, to take a sip instead of to answer a question. Then you only have to not say something for a mere second, and the conversation has moved on. There are countless new entry topics. Donations to charity auctions, funds committed to foundations, or juggling with turnover tax. Here, again, information does not help. Because the legal situation or judgments that have been passed down by the courts are not compatible with the lived reality and sense of justice of those who might lose something. Exactly the same applies to the illusion that 1
one is charitable. I am utterly and truly allergic to charity auctions. Artists are constantly being asked for donations to auctions for this or that charitable purpose. Why should artists gift their works? Is their output not considered a serious profession? Ostensibly, everyone else involved in the auction is working pro bono. And that's supposed to be true? A careful look at the books reveals astonishing allowances for expenses. For artists, gifting to an auction is an asset withdrawal and therefore not advantageous. The patronizingly issued certificate of the gift is worthless. But what the hell, it's for a good cause, and please don't look too closely at that aspect. Again, you'd only be the party-pooper preventing what was meant well. You can't overstate the case of there being a world of difference between well-meaning and well-done. The worst case for artists is if someone bids and gets a piece at well below the market price and then soon thereafter puts it up for public auction. The favorable entry level makes this possible for the person who obtained it in the charity auction. As a

result, the studio has to bid for the unfavorably gifted piece itself in order to support, if not restore, the original price structure. Because there is absolutely no way you want a low final bid entered in the database. The original bidder, by contrast, who purchases a work at a profit, can (if he waited a year) retain the profits free of tax, or so the regulations in Germany would have it. All of that for a good cause? An occupation with art is in no manner smoothly related to legal and tax issues. These jar in practice. And this likewise applies to private museums. In addition to all those reasons stated at cocktail parties, there's one reason for running a private museum that people dislike mentioning, namely that it helps you avoid tax. There are benefits for privately-owned but publicly shown art. This is less a daring statement and more plain knowledge gained by professional experience: With art, on balance you don't really save tax. Just as little as you can reap large profits with art. If one were to objectively tot up all the money and other resources (specifically time that here, as elsewhere, oddly is not treated as an asset) deployed to assemble a collection of art, one would only in strange exceptions end up with a profitable business model. Complex debates about whether you should enter the entire collection (everything you have bought) in the books and not just the super-items in order to arrive at reliable data on your own art investment simply poison the atmosphere. Collecting art has many positive effects. Saving tax is definitely not one of them. Meaning I expand the Swiss model for myself and propose that if you have the money to buy art and pay taxes, you are evidently in a good place. If everyone around me is in a good place, then I don't want to be the one who notices the fly in the ointment.

Being a consume is not a professio

Conversations that come to an abrupt halt on social occasions, with embarrassed faces all round, create lots of time to watch what is going on around you. It was this setting, with its blend of spatial proximity and distance in content, that enabled me in the past to garner insights into collectors: Collectors take time for art. They are free to go to an exhibition preview and travel to a fair, or not to do so. At the same time, they have something else and can do something else. For they have a profession, a job – at any rate a different life that frequently enables them to concern themselves with art in business terms. This, the other life of collectors, often remains in the dark in Operating System Art. By contrast, the professions pursued by the other participants in the art market are highly visible. A gallerist stands at a trade-fair booth, an artist is in her studio, a museum director holds an opening speech or is traveling, an author gives an interview or is seated at her desk. People who buy art pop up in all manner of conceivable art locations, and rarely does anyone know anything about their backgrounds. Sometimes collectors purchase over a longer period and repeatedly from one particular gallery, but information even on that is sparse. Yet the interactions with the collectors are somehow as if between close acquaintances. In fact, if someone requests a "collector's discount" from me as the head of studio and I then ask on what basis I should take a decision, I always get only very vague answers. This cannot be related to justifiable confidential business matters. Even the questions of whether this collector already owns other pieces by the artist or whether my artist fits into the collection for some other objective reason go unanswered. It is as if someone wants a collector's discount simply to confirm that one is a collector, and the gallery should fulfill this wish gladly out of concern that it might otherwise not make a sale. This does not sit easily with my duty, which is to keep an eye on the prices of the artist's works and to drive the prices. Prices have developed over the decades and are calculated after careful consideration. I will not deviate from that course without good reason. In order to avoid relapsing into my primary school phrasing and saying something like "you're crazy", I prefer to respond to such enquiries with a toneless "Oh". In other words, as if there were no Internet and the only source of information is a game of "Chinese Whispers". In the art market, suppositions are made that either have no substance or are plain wrong. Former gallery assistants who were paid in kind with artworks may evolve into important collectors. A baker became the world market leader in cough sweet production solely because he had the same name. One at best knows secondhand what one puts together to arrive at a person's biography and leaves it at that. In the art market, with its propensity for sensation, this will hardly have anything to do with discretion. Possibly, the market's opacity

derives from a yearning for proximity to important persons. When, many years ago, I heard a butcher rebuke one of his sales staff, I felt it corroborated what I myself thought. The salesperson had said: "The woman gets such-and-such." The butcher had made it clear to her that his customers were not women and men but exclusively ladies and gentlemen. It was key to treat everyone as illustrious. In the art market context, one exclusively has to do with ladies and gentlemen but not with clients. A gallery's clients are called collectors. The label sounds distinguished, and the client can feel esteemed. Because collecting sounds like a goal and like something having been achieved in life and not like goalless consumer consumption and profligacy. The entrance threshold is inconceivably low, as collecting can be merely a statement of intent. Anyone intending to buy the one or other picture in the future can immediately call themselves a collector and expect to be addressed as such. Collecting presupposes searching. Anyone who has nothing at home has perhaps not yet found the correct item. The unsuccessful search to date is a popular activity with a view to self-glorification.

More is more

When it comes to consumerism, in the general consumer goods cycle an advanced age is not an advantage. At the time when, assuming all goes as expected, you have the necessary readies, you have already exited from the groups targeted by classic advertising. In the art market in the West, things are different. Art dealers spotting young people who visit galleries and trade fairs assume they must be students and/or artists and therefore not clientele. The fact that we now have a young generation of people who have inherited wealth seems not to be widely known. The notion that inherited money is perhaps spent more readily than money you have earned yourself seems not to be something really considered in the market. If young people are not expected to have any money and/or not to spend it on art, then how do we explain that older collectors talk about having collected art for decades? This overlaps with the purported coup de main of the then "penniless" students. They started "with nothing" and "paid" for the art in installments through risky payment deals. When I asked whether the poor student simply took the first print he acquired home with him under his arm, the answer was: "The gallerist delivered the piece a day later as it did not fit in my Porsche." The contradiction between driving a Porsche and the destitute student was not obvious to the speaker? Accordingly, under the heading of self-mystification, there is always scope for coquettishly claiming not to be a collector but "only" to like art. At this point, what is decisive is the knowledge and/or imagination of those involved in the conversation. If they are not prepared to imagine some dream of a great collection hidden away behind the conspicuous modesty, then the coquettish gesture comes to nothing, of course. All these evocations of the good old days with art, fit as they are for a novel, are intended to prove the person's actual, sincere passion. And as a result, the super-rich have a tough time of it. How do they prove their passion if they can straightforwardly buy whatever they want and cannot cite hardship as proof of their dedication? For very wealthy individuals, the yardstick for the quality of a collection is tougher. Given their seemingly unlimited means, any interaction with art will invariably fall short of the great expectations held by others. Such envy of what others have often gets expressed in resorting to the claim that "less is more" when visiting the home of someone who basically owns everything. On such occasions, I say: "More is more."

> **Old age is like everything else. To make a success of it, you've got to start young.**
>
> Theodor Roosevelt

When I still worked in galleries, older clients always asked to be advised by the gallerist and were very miffed if they had to make do with me. I therefore made a virtue of necessity and attempted specifically to engage young people who visited the trade-fair booth or the gallery in conversation. First of all, they were happy to talk to me in the first place, and I assumed that they did not yet have firm links to a gallery and imagined that I might become their future main gallerist. Perhaps I also have a special relationship to time-in-life. Each year when the postman brings the latest law association pension scheme statement, I am delighted by the past years in which I have prospered and contributed to the scheme and start visualizing all the things I wish to achieve in my remaining years in the profession. In other words, I am an optimist who draws her confidence from the idea that nothing can dent my

pension. Which is why I so like what Roosevelt quipped. Because, seriously, the idea of an old age spent in poverty does not seem leisurely to me. At any rate, it is an advantage in the art market to at least be of middle age if you want to be served. The probability that you will get good information at an art fair or in a gallery rises with each wrinkle. Specifically, men with salt-and-pepper hair have very good prospects of being courted as collectors. If I happen to be unknown (my kids would say: Like when does that ever happen??) and a man is close at hand, then only he gets addressed, as if I were deaf and dumb or simply non-existent. Today, that doesn't bother me. Is the world changing? Do I still have any prospect of experiencing relevant changes myself? In Asia, or so the statistics of the auction houses show, a third of art buyers are under 30 years old. It will be interesting to see whether this impacts in any way on the behavior of European gallery staff. Will the art-fair format get a refreshing makeover and adapt accordingly? Will conversations at the fair change and the information 1.
offered by staff at the booths and in galleries be submitted to the stress test of online research? The statutory money laundering compliance guidelines have the potential to really disrupt things. If every client has to provide a copy of their ID, then at least their name and address are known. As an editor of the above-mentioned specialist legal journal GELDWÄSCHE UND RECHT, I am forever underlining the undesirable side effects of the money laundering compliance laws. Art purchases are not helped by the fact that, because gallery clients now have to submit their personal data, collectors' given names and years of birth are known. There'll be an incredible surge in the number of Jonathans. Whereas self-proclaimed Jonnys will swiftly die out. Suddenly there will be women over 50. Collectors may buy disturbing art, but they love wherever possible to be beautiful and important and mysterious. I knew all that and accepted it as given without pondering it too much. That was an easy move, as not only was my passport legit (the age was correct and the name in it said Sasa), but also I was not the one involved.

A shark in a pool of… possible sharks

Suddenly, however, I was myself subsumed under the heading of the indeterminate. I initially thought it was a matter of ignorance or a semantic oversight if I was introduced to people in my new private position, meaning at my husband's side, as a "collector". At times, I sought to rectify this misunderstanding (or so I thought) with an ironic touch. I suggested, tentatively, that a passion for collecting is not something you have from birth, as some might think, but is infectious. Or: If you marry a collector, then you automatically become one. Not that this is even halfway correct, as it is actually entirely incorrect. Conflicts in families stemming from the fact that the one person collects, and other family members do not
.9 want to see the resources drawn down by this passion thus squandered, are often cause to seek the professional advice I provide as a lawyer. The more time I spent at the collector's side and the more observations I made, the more blurred my view of myself. Public perception doesn't really help here and is not a good corrective. When I read in one of the Sunday papers that I had set out to redefine the profession of collector, I went back to bed aghast, as I found that so monstrous a distortion of things. The selfsame article accused me of being calculating and well-tempered. What on earth had happened to me? Into what had I, the former cabaret artist, now developed? What had happened to my sharp and poignantly explosive insights?

I had just participated in the panel discussion on "To collect is to consume, meaning spend money." In that light, how could collecting be a profession? Because a profession has the aim of generating the income you need to live your life. This insight relating to my working world, which in my perception of things cut through everything like a shark

Tobias Rehberger
HM → 134

Cologne Museum: Oliver Czarnetta, Konrad Klapheck, Tobias Rehberger, Tony Cragg, John Baldessari → 192

through a school of fish, had been overheard. Moreover, to resort to sharks again: That's Hirst, that's Britain. Let me defiantly adumbrate further on the profession of collector, only briefly distracted by the sharks of this world. I had only recently lectured that a hobby can be identified by the fact that one does not pursue it in corporate structures but alone or in clubs. There are, in fact, even special money-spending clubs. The sole object of such clubs is to spend money on art. Never heard of this? Well, think no further than "Friends of the Museum". The association's objective is to raise money to buy art. What the association's statutes actually say is fairly irrelevant here. Studio visits and other events serve solely to communicate the museum's acquisitions decision. Usually, an opportunity also arises to purchase something for one's private needs. These duty-free art outings are of course the nightmare of every gallerist. Because they usually involve direct acquisitions from studios, in contravention of all competition practices. Since all of this has been instigated by the museum, to whom one wishes to remain favorably disposed for a whole raft of reasons, the art business pro can often only gnash his teeth and snaffle his rage. As a court-appointed expert, I attempt to brand the direct acquisition from the studio as indicating erroneous provenance that will in due course come back to bite you. Sharks again. But my words of warning go unheeded. The seeming exclusivity and proximity to the artist thus proffered unhinge any questions of provenance that will, in any event, probably only bare their teeth decades later. It's simply too marvelous a moment when you buy something among the circle of other museum friends. All you need to do so is cash.

Collectors – the real pros in the art market:

A profession tends, as a rule, to imply having formal qualifications for it. Added to which, a qualified profession also tends to mean that it is something pursued over decades, regularly, to a certain degree systematically, and is something you involve yourself with to the extent that you go on training courses and obtain specialized skills in it. Is that true? An accurate description? In darker moments, I confess to myself that collectors on occasion engage in far more advanced professional training and networking than I do. While, as a lawyer and court-appointed expert, I have to work on the cases I have been assigned, collectors are free in their choice of object and can seriously immerse themselves in different approaches and research areas.

s collecting the new form of smoking?

Should I question how much of a professional I myself am because collectors whom I hitherto thought amateurs attend far more meetings than do I? Their seriousness, their ambition, and above all their culture of being present in galleries and museums' private viewings all seem highly professional. Collectors are always having to do something. Here and there and everywhere. How often did someone say to me gruffly, brusquely: You really have to have/buy/read such and such. Delete as applicable. My assessment that this activity seems overly driven and somehow anally compulsive behavior possibly says more about me than about collectors. My discomfort with sentences that contain the words "have to" and are supposed to have something to do with me remains unchanged. Because thus far I have lived and worked quite happily. If "one" simply has to do something because "everyone" does so, then frequently that's not for me. This does not affect the overarching principle. Off to Venice again, and now you also have to go to Copenhagen and to Ljubljana, too. Moreover, the pattern of not being able to let something pass you by, to want more and more, and to not accept that your family, friends, and acquaintances find your behavior off the radar – now I know all that. Because when you study law, you quickly learn to call the compulsion to repeat things while upping the dosage as the two pillars on which addictive behavior rests. The denial that yours may be problematic behavior does not, in the art world, apply just to specific individuals, but to the entire caboodle. Eulogies to this or that collector praise that "sense of drive". Indeed, collectors even position themselves by saying they have bought far more than they can afford, have overstepped the mark, have perhaps taken a gamble. It's a thin line dividing the admired role model from a pathological disorder. If you are, objectively speaking, operating in a highly complex system along with very many other players and in very many places, then the claim that you have gained an overview of things is quite simply the hallmark of megalomania. Even keeping tabs on a subsection of the whole is as good as impossible. I don't think it is laziness or negligence but rather a sign of maturity if I don't want to get a handle on everything, as that is manifestly unrealistic. If things are in flux, if things move along without the current washing you away, then you've already achieved a lot. Sometimes I cannot decide whether I should have a guilty conscience that I do not suffer from FOMO whatsoever, or whether I should simply say to myself that I chose my appointments with greater care. The more I had to do with collectors and got closer to them, the more I started wondering what the mixture of perfect self-PR, fiery passion, and social fitness was that I had before me. I used the tools of the profession I had learned, that of the law, in order to get to the bottom of this. The first step was to identify the matter at hand. I collected insights, compiled hypotheses, was astonished, and jotted a lot of it down in my diary as it came into my head, so as to later consider it in depth. Seen from the outside, it seemed to provide the stuff for a classic novel of development. Over time, I gained the impression that my role in the new context was on a trajectory that would culminate in what tends to be called a “fixed presence at the side of” someone. Now if that were a text message, I would respond with a “hahaha”.

Fixed presence

When I first met my husband Klaus, his private exhibition project was in the midst of decisive expansion. After several other locations and formats, his own museum in Cologne was ready. The soft opening had taken place, and now things were to start in earnest. The pleasant liminal state of merely imagining what it would presumably be like to fit out a room with art thus suddenly became a reality. Instead of rededicating an existing space and fitting it out anew, we were actually now confronted with the big solution: A building had been erected. I was not yet part of the planning phase. That at least gave me a fallback line, as I could complain about planning errors.

However, I swiftly grew tired of grouching, and with the massive effort and the immense courage required to take the limelight, I swiftly felt like a spoil sport. It isn’t fair to appreciate the fantastic architecture of other builds and then constantly complain that a private museum, which needless to say is meant to have an emblematic outward appearance, is not practical. I therefore undertook to act as I did in my job and be supportive and take my place in the ongoing project. I wanted now to match the standards I set for others; to recall things here: Work that you do not see has been done to completion. Service is invisible. How do you make yourself invisible if you’re out there on a silver platter? What should the eye-catching initial events and daily operations look like? The “hardware”, as it were, was in place: impressive, and in part still being finished. Namely a mighty modern concrete building with large, high walls. From the professional storage room in the building, the art was transported up to the exhibition halls. The storage room itself could easily have been a display cabinet in its own right, with very high ceilings and as bright as daylight. Nothing looked improvised. The empty transport crates themselves bore labels that resembled calligraphy. Helpful staff with sharp pencils behind their ears carefully placed their tools in lines in a way otherwise only witnessed at the dentist. I didn't like the building; I didn't feel at home there.

I liked the sense of order

Nothing new that one likes, one knows, that is familiar. To be honest, in my closet I also lay everything out in parallel lines and arrange the gloves by color. On the inside, my closets resemble stores. I suddenly realized: I not only want to fit out former stores with art, but actually to have a store. What is that supposed to mean? Should I rethink the idea with the gallery after all? Or have I still not got past a sales counter and children's toys? Or is it not rather a healthy investigation of our economic system? Actually, I think it in fact an approach that spares resources, as to my mind I always have a keen eye for what is already there and see myself as offering the complete range of wares. Irrespective of what is required, it's all there at hand and ready to be used: be it for the opera gala, the Hawaii theme party, or the evening watching football on TV. Back in boarding school, I already found it strange that daughters from very prosperous homes at times only had very rudimentary stocks of clothes. It strikes me as a lot of effort to then, logically, have to improvise. That back in my boarding school days I was considered petty bourgeois, and my luggage viewed as the heavy-duty stuff that weighed the proles down, was something I liked in a strange kind of way. As a child, I was allowed to iron handkerchiefs. They were placed in a special drawer, arranged by person. As a girl, I dreamed of giving one away as a token of love. As a woman, I succeeded at this quite spectacularly. As a girl, I moved as if I were certain that I would triumph. It stood to reason that in my eyes paper hankies seemed profane. An object bereft of romantic potential. I preferred to surround myself with things that intrinsically offered a promise of happiness.

Over time, I realized that you only have to nurture the eccentric in yourself tenaciously for long enough, meet the gazes uncomprehendingly and with no irony at all, and then you almost invariably emerge the trendsetter in the pecking order. I therefore went through all the things in my parental home with this in mind, and discovered all manner of media that were suitable. My father’s various pairs of pajamas certainly fit the bill in a big way. The same applied to my mother’s dirndl. In my student apartment, the set for serving punch took center stage. I copied quite a bit of what I had seen the nuns at school do. Men’s shoes and their working aprons, which, unlike my grandmother’s, had no pattern on them, were quickly absorbed into my canon. Certain mannerisms in my posture stem from a mixture of convent and ballet school. As a result, the debate on cultural
5 appropriation at times seems fairly opaque to me. When is a quotation an appropriation? When is it paying homage in line with copyright law and when is it a punishable offense? Who feels they are qualified to determine all of that?

The time after “Don’t fuck in the factory”

In other words, I encountered my husband after decades of training, standing as straight as a ruler, my hands at ease by my sides, and slightly indeterminate, but cheerful and looking him clearly in the eye. I was nevertheless not well prepared for the task. I had always avoided a relationship that also had a professional side to it, or at least concealed the fact. A whole bouquet of reasons spoke in favor of this approach. Not least, staging myself as an art fairy was something that was most successful “alone”. I was familiar with different formats of relationships, and I had a lot of experience working as a curator for a collector. The combination of the two worlds was new to me, however. The field was wide open. For Klaus and for me. We slowly felt our way forward. At times somewhat clumsily, at times pompously, and rarely very skillfully first time out. At the outset, my husband, with the attitude of a lord of the manor and his words dripping with significance, initiated me into his plans. He was socially inhibited, and his hifalutin plans contrasted sharply with that. A prolonged soft opening would presumably have been the right choice in order to get into the groove. Instead, at a point in time before I even existed within the system, a list of important museum guests had been invited to attend. In other words, no pre-season friendly but straight into the Champions League. The preparations for this special invited event were our first stress test. Klaus presented the plans from before my time to me, and evidently the idea was to find out at the presentation whether the concept would take off. When he started listing the details, I swiftly started switching off rather than thinking about the response he presumably wanted to hear from me. The lord of the manor explained his curatorial achievements with the hanging concept devised specially for the guests in question. I felt a bit shabby because everything I associated with it was negative. In my diary, I noted maliciously that the selection was such a matter of stereotypes that he might as well have glued cash to the walls. Moreover, it was clear to see that possession had not yet been truly taken of the building, as the formats and walls did not go together.

Never heard of Bourdieu?

Sure, people only collect for themselves. Investments are ostensibly not important. Sure, people don't buy with their ears but only what they themselves like, fully in line with their own tastes. Blah blah blah. I've heard it a thousand times. Well, dozens of times. Was he not perhaps a sociological copycat image, a blueprint for the "collector" type, after all? In my diary, I accordingly complained about what taste was being talked about here anyway and asked whether anyone had, for a moment, thought about the fact that taste is always the product of critical interaction with the world and is not simply a given. Never heard of Bourdieu? The simultaneity of incongruent sudden insights and gaping contradictions in argumentation functions marvelously in a diary, as everything gets confided to it. In reality, things have to be put rationally and logically. The diary is a great place to store trial madness and notions that cry out loud, so unjust are they. It is comforting to write without trying to censor oneself, without fearing possible consequences. In my diary, I played through the opening event at my husband's private museum in different variations, all of them sarcastic parodies: "May I cordially welcome you to the AnyOldThing Collection. Here on the wall, you see a group

that cost a pretty penny. We are completely independent in our aesthetic judgment and buy at all manner of fairs round the world and at exactly three galleries. At the fairs, we go to the three booths, drink a glass of wine, and then we've seen all there is to see." Sometimes I really miss cabaret. What a shame that in cabaret you need an audience that has had certain shared experiences in life. Jokes about the art market are always inside jokes. No one goes to the theater to hear them. Possibly, the art scene is beyond satire because simply photographing it is already so bizarre that there's no topping it. The question is thus academic. As said, there's no market for it. You learn in cabaret workshops that what you attack is what you describe. Why attack a doughty collector? Collectors are doing something that is highly desirable. They buy art. That drives things. If no art is bought, then no art can come to be. Remember, not only artists and gallerists live from sales to collectors, but three quarters of museum collections are attributable to private money. If I attack a collector, then I saw at the branch on which I sit. Professionally, and increasingly in my private life.

Don't trash your own life

Having really spoken my mind to my diary, gradually more moderate, circumspect tones took over. I had spent my entire adult life until that point in the art world. And all of that was to have been off the mark? I consequently cautioned myself not to trash my own life. The impact on my self-confidence would be awful otherwise! With an effort that went well beyond what was called for, i.e., with what was, at the time, a carefully and purposefully chosen field and subsequent long and intensive period of study, all I had achieved was to land in a world of unreflecting idiots? All amateurs? And I had chosen that? What did that say about my talent for happiness, something I so like to cite? Evidently, I was quite beside myself, and the thinking machine therefore kept buzzing away. The term for this is a problem trance: You get stuck with a particular aspect and can't let go, the way a dachshund gets its teeth into a slipper. Just because others didn't see the downsides did not mean I had to exclusively point up the darker aspects. My humor and my curiosity to grasp a fellow human being as a complex creature jumped into the breach. Thus, I watched attentively, at times from a friendly distance, at any rate as un-judgmental as I could be in the situation about this man who collected art. And I discovered a fire burning within him that I discerned to be warming and passionate, but also unpredictable and energy-sapping. I would have to learn how to live easily with this. I was attracted by light and warmth. Klaus's intense preoccupation with art and the enthusiasm with which he worked with his collection, although still a fresh widower, and that he was likewise very clearly not someone who was happy being alone – all of that touched me. On the other hand, my professional experience told me that caution was in order.

It's shitty elsewhere, too. → 134

Iv Toshain
I PRACTICE WHAT I PREACH → 135

Art market Darwinism

Because on both sides of art production, be it in a studio or in the collections, people who are not main players do not get treated with anything like nicety. When associating with creative persons (and since collecting is quasi-creative, this also applied explicitly to collectors), I found it more than advisable to always keep art market Darwinism in mind. I reduce it to the following: If everyone thinks only of themselves, then everyone has been thought of. In the course of my work, I had recognized that I can achieve the most if I take good care of myself. Self-exploitation and the hope that others would sit up and take notice do not go far, let alone last for long. It was a long path before I was able to claim my own space and ignore others. I felt grateful and humble once work no longer plagued my sleeping hours and I was able to start each day anew, full of verve and confidence. And it was a state I definitely wanted to ensure remained constant and that forever remained mine. On the outside, I kept my cards close to my chest again. For the players around me seemed to assume that highs and lows were the precondition for, or at least a compelling side-effect of, the genesis of their life's work. Not that I considered it problematic, let alone beyond the pale, to aim for a consistently high level of satisfaction. In a somewhat defiant stance, defending my emotional peace, I insisted I was not creative but a service-sector professional. That way, everything jelled for me. I didn't want to burn my fingers, and most definitely not to be caught in the smoldering flames. It seemed to me risk enough that I knew that artists and collectors per se are constantly in danger, or at least have phases when they are burned out. Working for someone who goes through the highest highs and the deepest lows is very challenging, but I was pretty good at it back then. I was reluctant to leave the comfort zone of that certainty. Now I feel uncertain when faced with the idea of being linked privately to an

illustrious player in Operating System Art. I was, truth be told, really alarmed and realized that until that point, I had made sure I had essentially stayed on the outside looking in: close to the action but in the final analysis not in the fray. It was not wrong to sell that as an advantage, as it did after all enable me to be very good at doing my work. Conversely, though, it would surely now get harder, as I would have no place to which I could retreat. The moment I got to know my future husband it struck me that my method of always only looking in from the outside was possibly a bit dishonorable. Perhaps I was not really taking things seriously with art? I was caught in a trap. For this inner turmoil was but one part of things. There was, in addition, the outside world, which on occasion came home with a punch. It was shocking to be caught in a situation in life that brought to mind a piece of light theater. For there were others wooing Klaus. He was the most desired bachelor of the year. Widowed and attractive on many levels, many very different women had their eye on him as part of their own future. 1
Initially I did not understand some of the aggression I was suddenly encountering. It took a while until I realized that I was in the process of extracting a very hot and very rare potato from the coals of the marriage market. My excessive fantasy didn't really help in this context. I painted before my mind's eye a picture of myself in garish colors as the cartoon figure the outside world saw: Thirty years the younger, the blond lady of fortune sweeps mourning collector off his feet. Looking back, it is fair to say: On the inside and on the outside, those first few months were awful. It's crazy just how much energy it took not only to keep standing straight with my arms leisurely by my sides, but also to remain standing firm and yet pliantly with both feet on the ground. "Firmly and pliantly" was what my ballet teacher called it. We young dancers were not supposed to be rigid, but to be able to perform any imaginable figure on the stage, starting from an energetic position at rest. It was not possible to achieve this basic stance in the new setting simply by letting time pass.

Talking about art

While we struggled for the outer form, the way we treated each other was clear from day one: Surrounded by the collection, we'd talk about art – and the world. The standards that I had until then always derogatorily castigated, and which, from my viewpoint, collectors with a huge dose of self-confidence constantly claimed as their own experience, also cropped up in my husband's narratives. At first, I accordingly accused Klaus of having reflected neither on his decisions when selecting items for his collection nor on his motivation for building his own museum. Conversely, he carped on at my "excessively intellectual approach to everything". However, we at the same time impressed each other with what were indeed original, unprecedented views. I learned something about the role of art in his life, and he willingly took on my

trenchant deductions, not least out of a joy in an excellent joust. Over time, we thus managed to leave the stereotypes behind us. We discovered areas in which we essentially were completely of one mind. The path we had respectively taken to reach that conviction might have been completely different. That was and is specifically the case as regards the law and taxes. I expect my client to focus on the matter at hand and accept taxes as an ancillary matter that you have to live with. From an in-depth expert angle, my husband does not believe in tricks or feints but is of the opinion that a skillful application of the laws with all due legality will produce the best and most reliable outcomes. At the end of the day, we agree that taxes cannot be countered with greed or trickery and that they most definitely are not suited as a way of making oneself seem more important. However mundane it may sound I am absolutely certain that a similar view on money matters is the key to domestic bliss. All too often, on visiting collections and studios, I had experienced regular bouts of tears and gnashed teeth when it came to various money matters. Incidentally, I notice this happens quite independently of the amount of money that is objectively available in each case. Acquisitions of art, investments in artistic projects, business relationships with galleries – these are all potentially explosive areas if you share your life and your money with a partner. In this regard, my husband-to-be and I, after a fact-finding phase, found complete unanimity. Those toxic recriminations about marrying a rich man are now of little consequence. We thus debated all the different aspects of approaching art, and specifically of course our respective professional dealings with the relevant issues, in my case my work as curator of a private collection and valuer of art. In half-jest, Klaus has been accused of marrying the specialist for his collection and that this was a bit too obvious a stratagem. I did in fact tackle the matter of his art professionally and got round eventually to researching the genealogy of his collection. Once again, the outer valuation and the inner stance were at a far remove from each other. I found it fairly romantic to be so interested in a person, while from the outside, the research project was considered overly zealous, if not indeed born of economic interests in how much could be made with sales. Yet it was in fact through the intense discussions on art that we started to converse with each other. The focus was no longer on great finds and heroic acts of purchasing. In what is a dialog that has now been ongoing for many years and has never ceased, and never ceased to be interesting, let alone become boring, the butt of things has been whether art is the expression of what it is to be human: yearning, searching, hoping, along with the ruptures, failures, and useless attempts. Seeing through loving eyes, you have no need to condemn anything (any longer), even if you identify it to be a useless attempt. As a result, how I treat people very close to me has changed radically: What counted next was just "chatting". There was nothing left for the eye to learn because nothing much happened on the outside. For me, personally, it was no longer about dexterities and daily work that was appreciated. A sociological new beginning. Unlike where I came from, where what counted were visible achievements and fondness for each other was expressed through shared productive labor, no one asked me now whether I was reading or working. The bond was now expressed by exchanging thoughts and ideas.

We felt like secret agents when we looked at ourselves through outside eyes. Because the cleanly separate referential systems of art got all mixed up in our case. The sales-boosting division between collectors and the art trade was annulled by our link. How to take the sting out of a setting defined by hegemonic knowledge? We simply combined the quasi-knowledge we had acquired separately from each other and talked everything through. Outside third parties who had in part known us for decades independent of each other suddenly found us hard going. Many didn't even know how to address us, politely or as friends. Many gallerists from whom my husband had purchased work knew me from my school days; they all treated me as completely familiar. The purported close ties that Klaus had to these gallerists was undermined by the fact that they chatted to me but were professionally polite to him. Objectively speaking, these situations no doubt had the potential to slight the narcissism of the one or other gallery owner or Klaus, or myself for that matter. Meaning to be an affront to all of us, and to the museum guy and the gallerist. We found the best avenue to take was radical openness by working through our encounters with other art market pros. Nevertheless, a few ties that had survived for decades went crashing down in flames. And the regret was limited. In the first few years, there was so much to be set in motion that at times we didn't have any energy left over to be annoyed by a business relationship with a gallery having been discontinued or a disastrous dialog during a preview. With more tranquility and circumspection, much could doubtless have been brought to a more successful conclusion, but the major issues required all our attention and effort.

It’s shitty elsewhere, too.

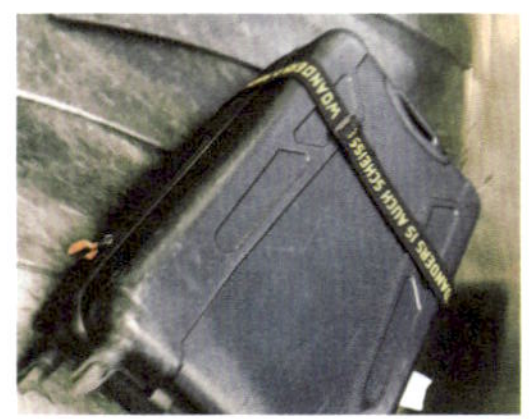

Elisabeth von Samsonow SASA,
Angela Glajcar, Tobias Rehberger, Prince of Dubai

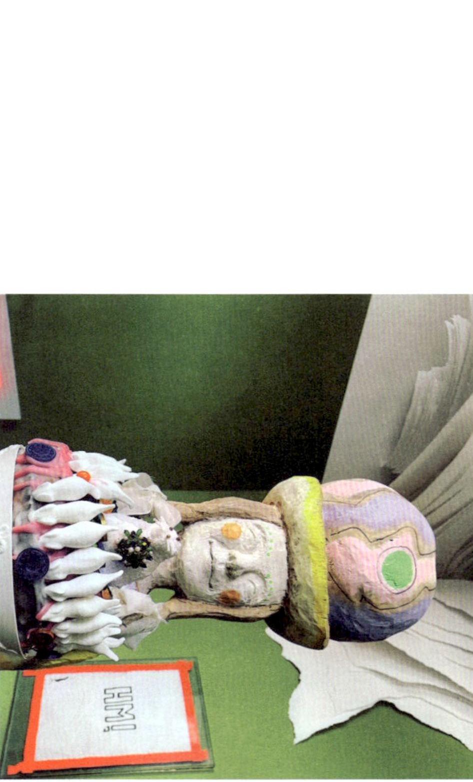

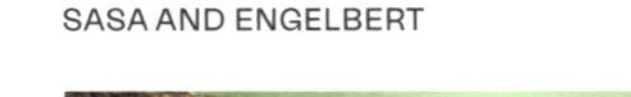

Markus Spatzier
SASA AND ENGELBERT

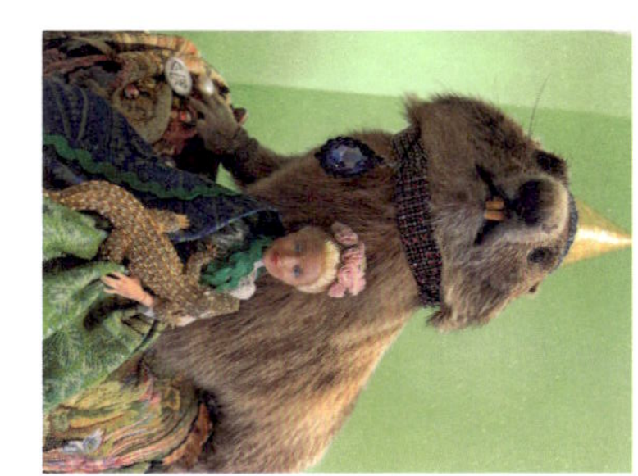

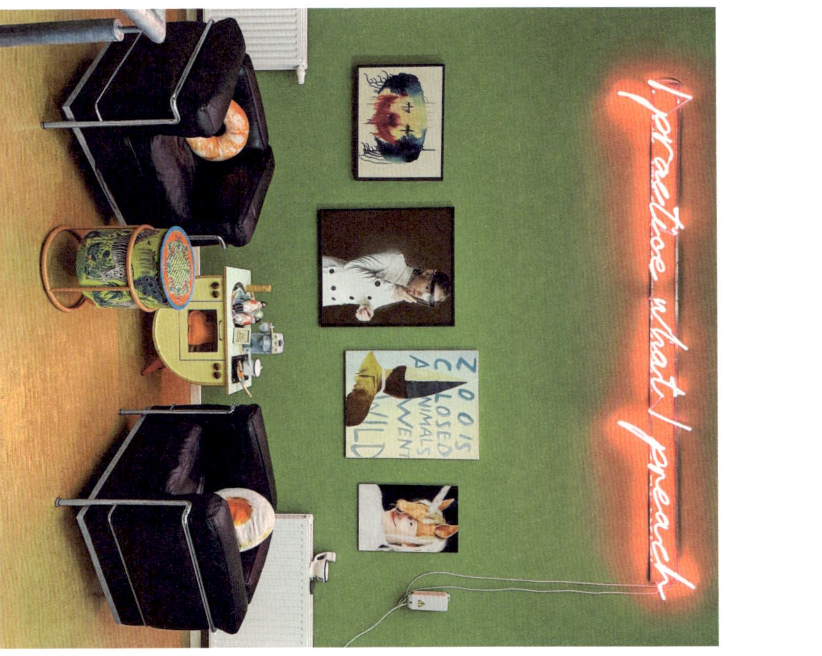

Iv Toshain, Sophia Süßmilch, Rosemarie Trockel,
Andrei Roiter, Claudia Holzinger

Rose Eken TEMPO
on the l.: Adaptation in the shop
window

Sleeping in the office

One of the toughest aspects was how to meld the two worlds from which we respectively originated to forge a shared life. Just as I had always dreamed as a child, I lived in the heart of town, while Klaus wanted to live with his art in his newly built house which was, as stated, to be operated as a museum, located in a suburb. Overcoming considerable inner resistance, I moved in with him. For me, living in a museum was a bit like having to live in a prosaic office. I was completely on my own on that one. Any attempt to discuss the topic with someone, to talk about my inner trepidation, got nowhere. Instead of support and advice, all I encountered were envy and miscomprehension as to how I could be so lacking in gratitude that I was able to have an abode in this huge, brand-new house. I resolved not to make a fuss of it, but to be productive and pragmatic. Hey, I would manage to conquer the house, or so I hoped. What then happened felt like pretty much the opposite. The house and the collection seized hold of me.

Infectious misfortune

The unusual misfortune of being a collector befell me. Completely out of the blue. The tricky feel for life that, seen professionally from the outside, I did indeed have and was reliably able to diagnose was in fact infectious. Once again, I was as isolated as the first-grader who hadn't been to kindergarten. It bugged me that no one understood why I didn't find it truly marvelous to live in this eccentric house with all the beautiful art. Just as architects have to rave about the dovetailing of inside and outside, I had to like the bonding of work and life. Yet all I wanted was the man, and not all the other stuff. The museum itself I did not like, although as an exhibition space pure and simple it would have been fine. As the center of my life, however, no; the house was bizarrely unsuited to me. How absurd, I constantly found myself thinking. Stating that all I wanted was the man did not go down well. I felt the statement was pretty damn romantic. All manner of different people responded to it as if I had told some dirty dad joke. As a result, I abandoned that line of argumentation. In substantive terms, though, that changed nothing: I did not want to live in a "chamber-cum-cupboard" with a view of a concrete balustrade (that for quite unfathomable reasons obscured the view of the garden behind it) in an echoing, public building. My man informed me that everything was simply subordinate to art. Now that I doubted, or rather everything seemed to be being subordinated to art without any thought at all. One could very easily have combined a museum with an appropriate home, even with a fashionable home at that. "I mean, it's not as though Peggy Guggenheim converted a beautiful, practical house in Venice," my mind kept telling me, aggrieved. I withdrew, studied, and found all manner of proof for my scathing judgment.

On the outside, I continued to try, tentatively, in a cultured manner: The liminal state of not having something and only being able to imagine it – that state has quite a bit going for it! However, irrespective of whom I presented the idea to that the greatest pleasure lies in anticipation, no one agreed. My resistance to my current situation living in an exhibition space was met with sharp rebukes, to put it mildly. The real bourgeois life was evidently a bit beyond me, the one said. Which only prompted me to retort: Maintaining a private white-cube exhibition space, and indeed the whole idea of a white cube, was petty-minded and uncouth. And given my prior studies, I had any number of arguments up my sleeve as to why the architecture did not add up to a successful emulation of Bauhaus. There were plenty of things to flaw.

I want to live happily

On brighter days, I tried to find something positive about the huge rooms; I really worked hard at it. What remained unchanged was the sorrow at past home settings in homes that had felt like a silk blouse. I wanted to be back living in rooms that embraced me like a hug. The museum was like an icy peck on the cheek. Somehow mendacious, emotionally twisted, something I, well brought up as I was, should allow to happen in company. My rebellious heart became louder and louder: “Is not the whole purpose of having a great financial reach that you can choose how you want to live?” I invariably got to hear the metaphor that I was living in a golden cage when conversation turned to my current life. The image was wrong! The golden cage is by definition in order; it’s just that you can’t get out. In this case, I could leave to go a-wandering or a-traveling. If you are like me and prefer to be at home, then a golden cage is not a problem. Some years later, my son Konrad was to remark that for me lockdowns and quarantines were really not a difficulty, as I was at home all the time anyway. The key thing in my eyes was that the cage was an echoing concrete box where you had no privacy and you couldn’t really work, because there was no Internet of the kind I like: everywhere, all the time, lots of it, super-fast. In terms of my preferences, the technical situation was in fact a true disaster. The most frequent opinion I got to hear from the outside world was, however, that I did not like the house because I was jealous of my husband’s deceased wife. Now that manifestly had nothing to do with me, since these objections did not relate to me as a person. I’m not even known for being jealous of people who are alive. In my case, jealousy and (as mentioned) a need for harmony, if present at all, are so marginal as to remain at a level beyond detection. Rarely does a person utter just one stupid statement. And thus it was that almost the very next sentence in such conversations was that I was jealous of the first wife anyway because she and Klaus had assembled the collection together as their joint life's work. The subtext was that a shared life's work, in my case, was impossible given the demographics involved, and I could read it like a bubble next to the mouth of the persons babbling so idiotically. Under the heading of "alternative dialogs", I would gladly have countered with a snappy retort. However, I usually didn't, not because I was too decent to do so but because I was too exhausted. It was all too dull, and for the first time in my life I was often fatigued. In substantive terms, I specifically rejected the notion of joint collecting by the Schmidt Couple, Version 1, as I term my husband's first marriage. My expert experience told me otherwise. Creativity and quasi-creativity in combinations of persons are something I generally view with doubt. In my opinion, you need a motive to collect. If my husband is the type of collector who works through personal themes in his collection and very evidently tried out and pre-empted entrepreneurial risks within it, then what

did his non-entrepreneurial wife then contribute? What had her motivation been? However, it was pointless to try and parry the collection being termed "joint", specifically as it was economically/legally the case; in fact, even daring to challenge it was quirky and overly intellectualizing. There is simply nothing you can do to counter imputed jealousy. I didn't bother continuing to do battle on that front. Which meant that I had at least preserved my talent for not fighting battles where there was no hope of success. So, I was not about to become the Donna Quixote of the marriage market of the rich and beautiful.

Finding a positive role to take

So, what positive role could there be for me? Is the collector's second wife a fixed role not dissimilar to the notion of a stepmother? A role in which, even if I were to play it to perfection, I would by status remain a second-class citizen –

no, that was not for me. In fact, I identified with that role to such a minimal extent that I thought, even if nothing really feels right here, before it simply degenerates into a problem trance, I'll simply get to work. Not that I ever forgot that Big Ben and the Big Apple look a lot better on postcards than they do in reality. And I steeled myself, telling myself I was one of a kind. Something had to be possible. I see myself as productive, and in my heart of hearts I am a titan of joy. I did not fall into hopeless despair and was not completely depressed either, but as a friend once commented when describing a particularly difficult phase in his professional life: I noticed I no longer sang under the shower. In close relationships I always knew how to put my finger on a situation in which someone wanted something from me – and I did not want to give it. The situation then was quite clear to me, and I could decide between a no (probable) or reaching an agreement, a balance. Giving something against my better knowledge, letting myself be persuaded to do it, tends not to happen. However, the situation in which I now found myself in life was one where I had no reference points, and I felt as though I were in a photo that was slightly out of focus and where, however much I enlarged a detail, it just became all the more blurred. Not enough pixels. I concluded from this that evidently I simply didn't know enough and that I needed to acquire greater depth of field to see the image properly.

Self-definition

As in good, productive working relationships, job descriptions do not become more precise until you start doing the job. Everyone then finds their place in the scheme of things. I, however, succeeded in this only in very tiny steps. I told myself that there would be a step in between and an effective inner reservation to it. Initially, I calmed myself by defining things defensively, saying that it was not my museum after all. The focus was therefore on the protagonist, meaning my husband and his collection. I didn't even feel I was letting him down, because even when he spoke of

"us" he was referring to the history of the collection, and I had not participated in it. As I was used to working as head of a studio, I again simply wanted to make myself useful. I tried to withdraw into the role of outsider looking in. Now receptions are an awful lot of work. And I therefore took pleasure in masterfully managing the organizational workflow, put my dress and apron back on, and withdrew into the role of lady of the house, or rather housekeeper. Whenever I was addressed with the wrong name, I considered it confirmation that all of this had nothing to do with me. Let my husband, the "chief" as he was meanwhile called, do his thing. Reality, however, then bit at several levels at once. In the framework of the agreements relating to our civil marriage, it emerged that I was supposed to be fully in charge from now on and forever more, meaning over and above the years we would hopefully be granted together. Hitherto, I had only been a service provider in other people's collections, and now I was to be completely responsible. And what
1 was even worse was that the chief didn't just "do his thing". He was evidently likewise uncertain of himself and didn't have a fallback plan.

A married couple opens an exhibition

Klaus quite clearly did not have a script for things in mind. I had uncritically deduced from his self-confident statements on the coming receptions that he would handle the content side of things like a virtuoso, indeed like the grand seigneur that he basically was. In over a decade of curating a private collection, meaning as a mercenary, I had learned that people did not like me asking questions about the content of the opening speech. If I'm asked, then I help; if I'm not asked, then I have to endure whatever the speech turns out to be. I had not foreseen that the armor plating I had placed around my soul in this context was something I would need for the very first event we hosted together. The guests arrived, the hall gradually filled. And Something happened. I'm always surprised in opaque situations just how many different distressing things I can think about all at once without, however, letting my panic show: Why isn't he saying something? Why hasn't he started? Why's he hiding and getting something from the basement instead of standing at the door? That's what you're supposed to do. Stand at the door, welcome each guest with a sentence. "Hello, great that you were able to make it." Always remember the name. Wait just that one moment until the photographer has hit the button. And then the next guest. Forever photogenic. Don't touch your head! Why's he not giving an opening speech? He took notes after all! And where have the notes got to? Oh no, surely, he's not going to ad lib? No, surely not?! Hope briefly flickers that he wants to emulate me and speak off the cuff. The best thing is clearly to leave your audience uncertain whether you are indeed about to speak off the cuff, have already made the same speech various times, or are simply really good at learning things by heart. My ideal is to be witty, charming, and to show complete mastery of the topic at hand. In a short and succinct manner. Kindling extra fascination. No safety net or backup. Meaning: no pages in your hand. No, nothing in your hands, as you use them to emphasize what you're saying, and if I then manage to establish eye contact, to take my time, to adjust my timing to the laughter of the guests, maybe even skillfully respond to any heckles, then it's more than good, then it's a mixture of pure "bubbly for the brain"– the three E's: effervescent, elegant, enchanting. This time round it isn't. As regards the before and after story, we're stuck in the before. It was ghastly for everyone present and it took quite a while until the disaster was digested. Looking back, it was hardly astonishing that in this high-profile moment and situation we performed a complete bellyflop. Opening your own museum is tantamount to an emotional state of emergency, the potentially explosive nature of which is repeatedly underestimated even by entrepreneurs who are accustomed to landing successes. My husband was out of his depth when it came to fulfilling his big dream, when crossing the demarcation line between that liminal state in his imagination and the lived reality. Added to which, there was now someone else at his side. It was all simply too much. In private, Klaus stated that he had always held all the addresses in the family, and in his company. Even long after he retired from active business life, he was still forever being asked to give speeches at festive occasions. And it had always worked out perfectly. Yet much time had elapsed and profound changes in his personal life lay between these glamorous and deeply satisfying evenings and the launch of his own museum. The ability to master a social and communicative challenge in a structured manner was at that very moment not something he had at his fingertips, as if he were trying to use a muscle he'd never trained. And Klaus had not envisaged this and was therefore caught unawares. He'd thought, just as we'd played through all the

aspects of the exhibition as hung together, that he'd now be able to describe it vividly and fit-for-purpose for the visitors in question. Instead, he managed only convoluted, brief words of welcome and was fatally clumsy along the way. The guests were put out. His remarks could only be read as meaning we'd been a couple for ages, and I had moved in immediately after the death of his first wife. A group of his business buddies might have accepted that or even appreciated it. The well-heeled couple whose younger days were well behind them were definitely not amused. In part, those present gave the impression that secret fears they had had themselves were now suddenly being expressed up front. What does your spouse do if you are no longer alive? Or, which would be even worse, they were starting to worry whether their own husbands had a second family on the side. It was utterly ghastly. And above all, I was furious that this gathering of people unknown to me was making me be disloyal toward my husband, because, as we had found out earlier regarding the collection, I had a clear inner barrier to what was going on. Anyone who is arrogant and refuses to let himself be helped will simply get a bloody nose, or so I wished. It would of course have been more fruitful to provide him with assistance, greeting the guests at the reception (the disaster could already be felt in the air), and to courageously jump into the breach. How admirable those women hosts who seem always to be alert. Helpers and children afterwards consoled me, saying it could have happened to anyone in my situation. Anyone, sure, but why me? I reproach myself: If you really know what's what, you don't get negligent. Perhaps it's because of decades spent busying myself with pictures that I imagine running an exhibition space to be like an image, a still rather than a film, a road movie, or possibly as documentary material with no editing. Unlike in a picture, a snapshot, openings in your own museum home are an arduous matter, a marathon in being on top of things. Timing is always a key issue. Even with subsequent, better prepared events, we were still all under stress, and the narrative about being quick-witted and sharp soon took a trashing. Later, I still found myself realizing in the middle of an event: I'm not on top of things. If you're the host, you can't go home at some point once the excitement's over. Retreat into your private rooms – now surely, no one would dare do that? Who simply lets things continue – and absents themselves? In fact, even if perhaps in some cases no one noticed, I always found events an emotional burden. They left me as washed out as a small child who, in the middle of a meal, suddenly falters, drops her spoon, and falls forward, fast asleep. The long sleep of the dead. Unlike the infant, I often didn't wake up refreshed but emotionally drained.

Post-collectable chill

Was that a new state of being? Was it really and utterly true that I only knew the collector's strange sense of trepidation from the outside? If I took an honest hard look at myself, then I saw that the pattern of being subdued and vaguely disappointed was something I was long familiar with, albeit from a different context. My emotional world relating to art fairs, exhibition previews, and exclusive dinners has repeatedly triggered flashbacks that took me back to the time when I was a child. Comparable situation in life: a children's birthday party. Because that's the key to children's birthdays? The excitement to see whether you have been invited, who else has been invited, who turns up, who doesn't, and who doesn't want to? Are you one of the special guests who get to overnight, too? Did you get the invitation late, meaning you were only second best, and got it because others didn't or couldn't take part? What shall I wear, who do I want to be on the day, whom will I be sitting next to? I imagine how I will win at pinning-the-tail-on-the-donkey, cut a fine figure at spin-the-bottle, and am of course absolutely best-in-class at the nocturnal karaoke session. Needless to say, reality often lagged a long way behind my expectations. Unanticipated complications so often got in between things! The carefully chosen dress gets grotesquely caught up around my legs because the trade-fair floor charges it with static; I get besieged by people whose existence I had completely forgotten and with whom I seriously do not wish to be seen; I get all mixed up in the middle of a conversation because my face is so tired I can no longer articulate clearly. And I cannot stand myself for inconsolably scanning the crowd for a face I like, for another person, and if, when I enquire with the gallery what the price is, I get treated as a lightweight and therefore no price gets revealed, then I want one thing and one thing alone: to be back in daydreamland. In other words, whosoever has felt unprotected and made to feel like a fool at a children's birthday party, at a trade fair or a private view, the way you feel when the zipper simply won't obey you just when the saleslady whips the curtain back on the changing booth, knows only too well what it feels like to open your own museum. The last time I felt as drained as after that first reception afternoon in our own museum was after a children's birthday party, and it was my birthday.

I had turned ten. Once everyone had left, I swore to myself that I would never, ever, ever feel that way again: empty and sad, and it was all my own fault.

How do self-made traps work?

The very preparation of the art presentation, which the snobs delight in terming curation, provides the first indications of just how high a point the later emotional crash will come from. Because during the hanging, we were already asking ourselves whether the grand ideas that had just been so very tangible before our minds' eyes would really survive the road test. We brashly spoke on another occasion, namely when meeting friends and in company, of the collection as a pool of ideas. Artists gather objects around them, such as newspaper snippets and amusing figurines, that are supposed to function as a pool of ideas and inspiration, and we thought the storeroom could have the same function for us. Which was why the storeroom had to be not in the house and instead somewhere else in a hall of its own in a commercial park or, for that matter, in some forwarding company warehouse. That said, how often did we not then find ourselves standing in the storeroom, at a loss, completely uninspired? Charlie Chaplin: We think too much and feel too little. Nonsense. We're not even thinking but behaving like debutantes in front of a whole wardrobe full of gala gowns, none of which fit the bill. Incidentally, constantly lived practice certainly doesn't make any of this better; in fact, the opposite seems to be the case. After the first private view in your own house, you simply know how ghastly it can be. That hands-on, zestful naivety of the first take is over and done with. The censor in your brain takes the reins, and your thoughts stomp their way forward like a Rammstein song: How to do something really well and how to visualize it, if it is to survive more than the very first moment? Now what was the deal with data privacy law again, and the fees for the copyright association, and then the images of the glamorous events posted on the Internet? The good news is: Usually there are no incredibly great photos taken of the reality of the private view. It would seem that the mind immediately turns events into daydream memories. The museum as a monument in its own right, as a monument to your own importance – now that is what the Instagram account is to the well-meaning, latte-macchiato-sipping mother of none: A staged life for one's peers. Photoshopped, optimized, highlighted with Insta-glitter and Insta-glam. In a world richly populated with other people's images, you race to keep up; you have to, you have to get ahead. Everything is supposed to be effortlessly perfect high-gloss, and you have to fight to lead in visualizing just how marvelous life feels in the art world. People have corresponding expectations of the photos from such events, meaning that something like concentrated emotion will be visible for all and sundry. Everything is in place in your head. The house looks glorious. The carefully caring arrangements of the furniture, the tables, the necessary items, and the excessively special, oh-so individual objects all meld in a magnificent tableau of self-orchestration. So much for the imagination. When we sifted through the photos after the event, the great expectation soon came crashing down like a soufflé taken out of the oven that critical moment too soon.

Cameras don't gaze with loving eyes

A WeTransfer can ruin your whole day. Expectantly, you unpack the huge data package the pro photographer has uploaded for you. Curiosity killing us, we sit in front of the large screen. Ouch! In the technically pretty-much-perfect images

(there's no shifting the blame, here), it pretty much looks like we'd hung up holes. The art seems lost and tired on the powdery gleaming walls. The works seem to drift helplessly on them. Power sockets are another issue. When you're using a house as a home, they're forever in the wrong place, either inexistent or too few of them. The photos showing the exhibition speak a different language. From the power socket via the light switches to the smart house systems. The facilities technology is omnipresent and impossible to overlook. Not that it seems particularly futuristic; rather, there seem to be cables running here and there for no apparent reason. The building seems somehow improvised; in the photos, the white cube of a museum looks like a garage: miserable rather than purist. At best functional. Meaning I'm left with just about zero, says my gut. What I'd wanted was to be rewarded for having given up the salon atmosphere in which I so gladly live and accepted that the museum building-cum-home could not be fitted out that way whatsoever. Now I'd felt I was being brave and reason- 1
able with my plan of not living in opposition to the house but instead finding a modus vivendi with it. The photos said something different. Nope, there was no point. At a local street party, I'd heard someone refer scornfully to our expensive exhibition building as a "junior high", and here I now was thinking maybe the guy had been right. In the pictures, at any rate, it seemed pseudo-modern, awkward, and somehow undesired.

In discussions about whether photography is an art, I always defend photography. However, viewing images in which the scene is attributed to me alone, and the photographer was supposed to document this, is to expose yourself to the veritable physical experience that transporting a photo, an idea, a feeling, a message is a tricky matter. We are not photo-artists. We don't manage to transport our idea of a highly personal exhibition that is capable of touching others' hearts, too. We don't even manage to produce good documentation to show that others took note of the exhibition. When in use, the champagne bucket filled with kitchen utensils looks pretty neat and introduces a different feel to a house that is otherwise squeaky clean. In the photos, it looks like some abject item from a flea market, mixed with things that would best be placed in orderly fashion in a drawer. I had Eileen Grey before my mind's eye; on the screen, everything looks as if it had been shot by smartphone in a large furniture store just off the interstate ramp. The images showing things that are otherwise not there and were only there for the event are as good as unbearable. The crates in which the pretzels were delivered try and take pride of place in one image; there's a shopping bag in which a guest brought a gift along, and plates with a few leftovers on them in the non-picturesque version and instead on the sideboard below precisely the one hanging that we mulled over for an entire day. Dingy and depressing. And it's not just the world of things that is anything but gladdening to the heart. The guests and (far worse still) we ourselves look a hell of a lot less "impressioning" (a marvelous word coined by artist Bernhard Martin) than my memory would have it. What's the term for a "bad hair day" if it involves your whole body? The best, most emotional photos are invariably, how could it be otherwise, of the "wrong" people, meaning those guests whom someone brought along with them and of whom no one knows the names, or of people about whom, when you see them in the shots, you ineluctably think: not really my favorite. Why are we all so puny? Why are we standing around as though we were collectively lost? Why the distance between the two of us in the shots? And in the rare photos where everything else is right, someone inevitably has a glass in their hand. Seen in the harsh light of day, that doesn't really fit the image we wish to present of ourselves. It takes a while to metabolize this severe narcissistic injury. In that telling moment of experiencing the fact, it is of course hard to countenance ever getting over this, but we of course eventually do. A loveless, nothing-to-do-with-us cataloging of things for the archive helps to boost the act of forgetting, and suddenly we're back in the race. Onwards to new projects. Now that is in line with the personality profile of a collector: forever diligently endeavoring, seeking out, hunting down. Ever onwards, ever upwards. Next time round it'll all be different. That post-collectable chill is like lovesickness, I then tend to explain: six weeks of physical pain, and then you no longer know what it was all about, why it was in the first place. As cultivated persons, we all want to grow with our experiences. And thus, correspondingly small tweaks are made in that is that. A few things are decorated differently, and the outermost edges of the one or other principle are revisited, according to which tablecloths are kind of nice, and after all they are sound absorbers, the photographer needs to be better briefed, or the like.

Making yourself Instagrammable

The selection of the art and how it is hung are toyed with over and over again, ready for the next display for the outside world. How difficult a private hanging is compared to distributing art in a gallery. In the professional context, the exhibition space is predefined and the goods finite. What gets hung is what is released for sale in the gallery. In the case of an exhibition of works from a private collection, the possible range is large, the topic open, and in the moment of the hanging something always seems to be missing. Vacillating between the poles of "surfeit" (shelves are full) and "dearth" (if we'd only bought the Sherman "Clown" back then as now we "only" have seven other pieces). In a private abode, the art on display is intended to resemble a snapshot from our everyday lives with art. The exhibition is supposed to be like visiting friends. The main thing is supposed to be conversation, friendly interaction, inspiring chats. Art and the building are meant to function as the outer envelope supporting all this. And these emotional moments are supposed to be recorded in order to foster further communication. How to render a successful evening visible? Well, hairdressers and restaurants tend to have an Instagram corner. There, everything is in place and duly lit such that it looks grand in a photo. At weddings and festive family gatherings, you sometimes get photographed inside a frame. Which I find deeply embarrassing. To my inner eye, I always look like a complete idiot, namely banal. Yet all the images shot of such an action taken together then look different. The average photo is really good. I take this levelling function of planned photo settings very much to heart. I simply swallow my vanity. In light of this insight, I notice how I walk around the house looking for the planned photo angles. Never again a photo in front of the shoe rack or the elevator. Because the house looks like some basement done up for DIY or alternatively like a meat factory. What we need is a canonical photo location. Then we can take it from there. After all, the photographer's briefing is also part

of things. First up, or so a further merciless autopsy of what went wrong reveals, we need to remember how we ourselves look, as one eye half shut can be photoshopped away, but the shame-filled poses of the collectors cannot. Meaning, no more crossed arms or fingers on a chin!

“Nothing is tougher than visualizing ‘authenticity’”

Alongside art and good catering, your own appearance is of course also a key asset. What to wear in order not to be dressed in an overly quotable manner but so that, if asked, I don't have to drop any names that would not fit how I present myself? Honest self-diagnosis when assessing the complete range of possible options shows: My interest in fashion is far too refined for the purpose.

My wardrobe only contains items that outside observers will simply not understand, not in the depth and density in question. Deconstructed. Feminist considerations on my silhouette, reflections on seamstresses' traditions, borrowings from Pop culture, satirical commentary… All of which spells: an end to this stubborn habit of indirect intricacies. I put my pride in the precious robes and disguises I have assembled down through the decades, my armor as it were, to one side and view myself through the eyes of a PR agency. The good news for the couturiers was: new purchases, expansions to the range, and a new invention all translated into considerable outlays. For the first time in decades, what played a role was what I looked "good" in. Since the museum entered my life, the emphasis is no longer on the robe as an art form and as demonstrative reflection on consumerism, but on chasing after hitherto firmly scorned standards such as "normative beauty" and "attractive". It was something that others would quickly discover and which would be commented on specifically by men with phrases such as: "Actually you were always a beautiful woman, but now that you have money the new look really brings out the best." I felt too clumsy to comment on how expensive the "architect's clothes" had been. After all, I'd always had the reputation among the rich guys of having no standards at all. "You with your Amish nails and convent shoes, you're cheap to maintain, I mean you don't even want a car." Remarks on economic conditions and your own approach to cash are generally dodgy, so I limited myself to keeping the ball in play with "something about what you just said was somehow unclear, what was it you actually said?" Usually, in such situations I resorted to activating my lotus skin and just letting everything wash over me. In films, it is music that creates the emotions without the viewers really noticing the fact. A photogenic, quotable look would underscore my masterfulness and expertise. However much I liked the eccentric look I had played through in countless variations until then, I told myself that in the eyes of others I looked like a freak. Peggy

Guggenheim pronounced that in Venice you can wear anything without appearing ridiculous. Cologne is not Venice. I like people; I like success in people. I did not want to artificially restrict my opportunities. When Rosemarie Trockel recently dressed me as a widow for one of her tableaus (p. 42), it became clear to me that another consideration also played a part. I didn't want to look like a widow. When you're 25 then exclusively dressing in black is a possible approach at all sorts of levels. I had defined the time for change well in advance, among other things out of fear of missing the right point to get off the black bus and become a dotty, sad old bird. As regards fashion, changes can be swiftly implemented with a little knowledge of the market and dexterity, and it all depended on me, anyway. Other aspects of life that relate to outside impact are harder to influence. I scanned the house for corners where the dirt collected. Nothing is more of an effort than imagining nimbleness and "authenticity". And insinuating quality likewise requires inputting a lot of energy. Specifically, it was key that the house did not look like an image from a furniture catalog, but everything needed to be high-grade, chosen knowledgeably and with a feel for form. Only recently, a holder of one of our foundation's scholarships diagnosed that I speak like a man. I had almost forgotten the fact, and now I remembered that in the past someone had said something similar to me. On this occasion, the conversation was all about decorations. Evidently, I was finding things stressful and swiftly became sharp-tongued if the house was not swiftly and thoroughly enough transformed into something "Instagrammable" and able to hold its own. It was not only the coffee-table books that fell victim to my attack. In particular, candles and bouquets of dried flowers were immediately shown the door. In comedy sketches, married couples argue forever over toothpaste tubes that have not been squeezed correctly. Today, I know that if your spouse wants bric-a-brac whereas you prefer an uncluttered desk, then you need to tread softly and be prepared to compromise. Who was to say what was right en route to staging our life with art? We received a highly instructive lesson in all things relating to home staging from a quite surprising side.

Murder on the patio

Suddenly, a slick gent with long hair was standing in our house enthusing about it being the perfect location. Perfect? For what? In his opinion, he had found the perfect location for a wealthy, highly neurotic, and affected killer. The latter would make the ground floor home to his sword collection, practice a form of Asian martial arts in the garden, and then go out to murder. We agreed – the result of a very crude mixture of self-irony and a zest for adventure that was somewhat mercantilist. The fact that everyone we told of this was horrified and tried to urge us not to do it only served to urge us on. We were inquisitive and sensed an opportunity in the outside view of the house. And our hopes were not dashed. A few weeks later the crew arrived and about 50 people occupied the house for a couple of days. At a word, all their movements and talk froze. In the most confined of shooting scenarios, the persons behind the camera stood or sat without making a sound. Why is that not possible in concert halls or in schools? They were busy, concentrated, often for many hours on end. Everyone on set was enchantingly friendly and confidently relaxed, even if now and then there were clear problems. It was a joy to watch these pros go about a craft quite unknown to me. When did I last learn so much in such a short time? The entire family was quite astonished that, bar the one or other piece by Angela Glajcar, absolutely nothing of the house's contents was used. Nothing. Each scene was completely furnished from scratch. New walls were erected in front of the concrete walls, new cupboards, simply everything. For me, the furnishing looked, to put it mildly, completely out of place. Somehow old-fashioned. I commented on this to the on-set director, albeit indirectly via a somewhat poorly witty remark: "Oh dear, the neighbors who only know the house from the outside are now bound to think that we once had an entire discount furniture store here." In an unforgettably masterful and professorial style, she explained to me: "We fit it out the way our audience imagines rich people live. Your reality is far too far removed from that." In other words, my sartorial decision was spot on. If you're too far removed from things, you are a freak whom no one understands. The set director impressed me a second time, on the very last day. While people who have known me forever still insist on gifting me chocolate (I don't eat it) and tea (I don't really like that either), she thanked me for my hospitality with a very large slab of venison; she herself had hunted and shot the deer. Never before was someone so touched by a piece of meat laconically packaged in shrink-plastic. As all the film-set stuff was packed away into vans and disappeared, we found we liked our own stuff more than before. We did, however, buy the carpet the TV people had laid from them. We had the feeling that we now had the best of both worlds. Even months later, I still found myself hoping that I would bump into strangers in the kitchen the way I had during the shooting. I really missed the days; they had felt so much like being in a dream flatshare. I consciously stored that feeling. Where would I be able to find it again?

The impostor syndrome?

At any rate, during our events this pleasant feeling of friendly interest in one another and of an apposite exchange of ideas failed to arise in anything like regularity. It flickered up now and again but did not define the tone of things. There was no rewards system in place. Artists and gallerists can at least experience sales as a simple form of recognition. Conversations at the fair or in the gallery are of course stored to memory as a potentially good business or otherwise career-supporting contact. In a private museum opened without any intention of turning a profit, there was no scalable parameter for success. And since, moreover, we had no regular opening hours, success could not be meaningfully measured in terms of visitor numbers. Being together as a family after an event also caused other irritations. At times, we got the feeling we had each of us attended a different event. And the photographer who was supposed to document things "casually" felt the same. However hard we looked, the good moments that my husband, the children and I had each for ourselves experienced were not to be found in the photos. We uneasily watched how our own museum took hold of us. What had we presumed we were doing? Was this an example of the impostor syndrome, or were we simply in fact not modest? We did what we could do best: We talked to one another and explored the available information as best we could. When, at one point, we were sitting dejected on the sofa again, the children became abundantly clear. Jakob and Konrad had sacrificed their school-free Saturday for the event and had dressed up smartly. Although they hadn't really been told they would have to, they were expected, if necessary, to help out. Konrad (seven at the time) summed things up by saying to me: "I made you an espresso specially. And then one of those people said to me: 'Ach, great, a nice espresso.' So, I made him one, as well. And another few people came up to me. I made them espressos as well. Two people gave me tips. I made 40 Euros. In our own kitchen! It was crazy! I didn't know what to do. I couldn't say no, could I? I'm sure they meant well." My inner reaction was as troubling at so many levels as the entire day had been. It was supposed to not have been an effort. It was for Konrad. Hosts, not derogatory towards guests, unreservedly open, friendly, and generous. And we adults? Is it snobbish or pseudo-feudal that we do not want to work with wage-earning occasional waiters, but that the staffers who belong to the house are in charge, and depending on the event everyone who is part of the household helps out, and of course no one gets a tip? It wasn't abundantly clear that the children were not expected to work in the narrower sense. Is there a right or wrong? Is there a rule hidden away somewhere in Debrett's? Must children wait on others? Is it alright if children do wait? Should we pay them for their labors, or is that simply a family duty? What were those people thinking dolling out tips? Is that perhaps just completely normal? What relationship do we actually have to money? And what is the children's relationship to it? At any rate, Konrad's attitude was completely unconcerned. He thought the adults were "correct" to act the way they did, as if they were in a hotel, and to sit down leisurely on our family sofa. Elsewhere I have found fault with the fact that children do not like their parents' collections and feel the art to be estranging, indeed to be in competition with them. Children have that extra enzyme that allows them to detect the lies in their parents' lives, I then pronounce. The parents may play at being so socially committed, but actually it is greed that drives them to events. Craving importance, from pole position they storm the gates of the fair, the preview, the pre-preview… Had the same now befallen me?

Diagnosis: emotional art market idiot

It cannot be that a harmless reception, meaning an event that was supposed to seem casual and easy-going, goes buzzing round my head in such a way! But that's what happened. This part-paranoid dent to my mood bubbled up in me with constipated regularity, or so I recorded mercilessly in my diary. The old rule that it is not motivation but good habits that lead to success also functioned in this instance. The view as if from the outside, through writing things down, was slowly to uncover what the solution could be. So what lay beneath it?

Your own museum – a castle in the ai

The post-mortem: The question as to what it actually means to maintain a private museum was only raised in relation to some of the aspects of it that can be addressed objectively. In my work as a court-appointed art expert and lawyer, I frequently encounter this model. While personal presentation spaces are planned, an association or a foundation gets set up, and the legal and fiscal angles get discussed, but there's never any precise discussion of who will run the day-to-day business. Even when it comes to acquiring an archive program for the collection or concluding art insurance, the issues of manpower, data updates, and handling are never really thought through. What tasks are identified, what possible problems imagined, and what personal advantages are hoped for all say a lot about how 1
the collection will be treated and managed. Often, things get collected for imagined third parties (Michael Cahn in MERKUR, 1991, no. 45, p. 687), and things are exactly the same with the museum. The one museum founder wants to give something back to society, the other has many works to put on display. The target group consists of art-interested fans, cultivated people, with whom inspiring conversations may then ensue. A salon may then be established, with regular soirees, but also with ramblings that result from the narratives of some good old days that are shrouded in mystique, but which the actor him or herself never personally experienced. For even the museum founder was too young, was too old, was in the wrong place or too busy to accumulate the financial resources now being used to set up the museum. In her mind, the castle in the air of her own museum is busily being furnished in advance: Museum founders have "so many themes for exhibitions that cannot be held that way in public museums, which are basically never sufficiently daring" and are subject to finan-

cial constraints and hierarchies, all of which is “naturally quite different” in a private museum. The invitations would be produced by renowned graphics designer X, who was the current flavor of the month, and the catering provided by Y, but who will handle updating the database for the invitations? The imagined guests are an anonymous mass of claqueurs. Where to find them? Remember that song about taking it easy and lightening up while you still can? This is what the uber-father-like museum founder conveys, withdrawing behind his newspaper. Founders, foundation patrons, and entrepreneurs love playing a role where they don’t need to concern themselves with tomorrow’s details or the nitty-gritty of things; instead, they devote themselves to the BIG questions that need to be solved before the museum opens its doors for the first time. The plot of land, architect, facilities technology (security, a turnstile, a cloakroom with lockers, a storage space, a legal structure – letting the building out to the foundation that first needs to be established, grants, etc.). Seemingly everything has been thought of, the professional dishwasher, the 150 champagne flutes, the chairs, the lectern and microphone, so that even larger groups and the garden can clearly hear the wisdoms pronounced with such sonorous charm. My experience when counseling clients on how to make bequeathals and when compiling expert opinions on arguments between heirs has been that collectors know little about the motives and view on life of possible successors. Rather, the presumption is that the heirs will be delighted to be “worthy of the inheritance” – or so a client once proclaimed. When translated into the terms of private exhibition operations, this means that a well-mannered, conformist, and reverent behavior is expected of the heirs. After all, one is a guest and is being admitted to the delicious seclusion of the private museum.

Doll's house Demented relationship Betrayal of love

Just as I must have seemed wooden and moody as a child when watching grandmothers spreading butter on a piece of bread like strange, half-way cute animals, so, too, I never shed my impression that here, adults expected of perfect strangers that they would be amazed with wide, glowing eyes, like children in front of the Christmas manger. Cognitive dissonance. I felt ashamed. The post-mortem result was tough: Doll's house. Demented relationship. Betrayal of love. So let's go through it step by step. On the doll's house: It may be different in other sectors, but in art it is standard practice for professionality to be a constant object of discussion. I have never heard that when somebody wants a new balcony door installed and someone turns up in overalls cheerfully saying "What carpenters can do, only carpenters can do" that anyone started doubting that a skilled tradesman was now at hand. There's coffee and small talk. No one asks to see the apprenticeship or master craftsman's certificate. No one says to the carpenter that the carpenters in New York and Berlin are cooler. And you don't say you're halfway a carpenter yourself simply because you have a measuring tape at home and have managed to glue a doll's chair back together. Since you've often watched carpenters at work likewise doesn't mean you think you know exactly how it all works. Just as you are not about to suggest that everyone is essentially a carpenter and, given a little time and an opportunity to drop by the DIY store, can do carpentry. Nor that the price is far too high. Let alone that it's such a great trade that the activity itself and the honor of being able to work for a super employee is reward enough, particularly as the work could be used as a reference piece when approaching other clients and therefore there is no need to be paid for it. Confrontations with this mindset in the art world are not some satirical exaggerations, but my daily bread. After decades of working in the art market and with a series of relevant professional seals and graduation certificates under my belt, why is my professionalism being fundamentally doubted? Because you are always thought to know about art if you say the amateur before you is right. If you differ, then your expert knowledge is called into question. Accordingly, the art market players carefully make certain that they stand out as professionals. It's now decades since a lady declared that it was simply a case of a mule accusing a donkey of having its own shortcomings. I am constantly reminded of that sentence. One gallerist accused another of simply playing at being a gallerist. There are no limits to being mealy-mouthed. And people close ranks if others become active in seeking to lay part claim to the area they have staked as theirs and only theirs.

n matters of taste you're always right

Collectors are denounced for being dealers and smiled down on for their poor taste. Or at any rate those who do not buy in your gallery. Bad taste, never had it. And bad behavior? The same applies. Even before our museum opened its doors for the first time, repeatedly guests did not behave with the good manners my husband had come to expect. A striking example of this was a guestlist a museum had submitted in advance. We were not given the guests' names, nor were they entered on the list with some other flattering attribute. The Word document was entitled

"Dinner Sunday". Then all these people turned up with their backpacks, their shopping bags, and their dirty shoes. It was a bit as though we were being paid a visit by the two highwaywomen from Heathrow – with 60 other like-minded persons. Anyone who does not want to become a restaurant manager, or a hotelier should not open the doors of their house to strangers. So, the bathroom needs to be repainted after being used for a reception with 62 curators? Anyone who can't put up with this without complaint should lock the front door. After events, we were forever finding half-empty wine glasses tucked away behind books in the library and bits of leftover food stuck between guest hand towels. What was the meaning of this? Was it the product of aggressive envy of wealthier people, or was it nonverbal communication saying that the person had seen through the game we were playing? These things went round and round in our minds, and it took forever until I, at long last, realized what the bigger picture was. Which is strange, because in other aspects of life I readily form a picture on which I then pass judgment. I could never have studied medicine, for example, simply because I don't look good in white, or so I told my friends. In reality, I didn't want to confess that I did not like the idea of working away from home among lots of other people, let alone having to do night shifts. Furthermore, it was abundantly clear to me that I wanted to have kids. Voicing such a topic at the age of 19 was completely out of the question.

Some things grow relative over time. I gave white a second chance. But in many other respects, I was right. The potential for a private museum inflicting one narcissistic injury after another was great. My husband apparently didn't notice this, or simply didn't know what it meant. During my jobs at galleries and art fairs and in my free time as a student, I had seen enough clubs, flat-shares, and parties.

Thomas Kiesewetter PORTRAIT, Clegg & Guttmann PROJECTION PORTRAIT (PEGGY GUGGENHEIM AND MAX ERNST) → 178

don’t need magination. ’m experienced.

In other words, I set the bar low from the outset. I was happy if it was only the toilet for guests that had been trashed by the evening and if, come morning, there was no one left in the exhibition rooms who was not resident at this address. As a child, I had had a doll’s house post office, complete with rolls of stamps, date stamps, a letter scale, and all the other paraphernalia. To now act as if we were museum directors, curators, press officers, janitors, registrars, event managers, temping waiters, guest speakers, and of course me as the trophy wife – that all seemed to me to be like playing with the doll’s house. We sealed the envelopes, franked them, sent them on their way, but none of them ever arrived in the real world. While a student, I had a favorite song; it was by the Yeti Girls and there was a line in the lyrics that went: “All your money seems to be a color-copy”. When our private museum opened its doors, I caught myself wondering whether anything we did needed to arrive in the real world. What I was certain of was that if we were to play the game, then it should most definitely be fun to play. Whereas on the day, the game felt like anything but fun.

There seemed to be a variety of causes for the discomfort. I had lived my whole life until then with the goal of not thinking, when in a restaurant, that I was sitting at the wrong table and the people opposite were having more fun. Anyone who came in should bring joy to my heart, and I didn’t want to feel as on edge as a young girl waiting for her first date. I felt shabby, not looking forward to the fact that “only” strangers were coming. Who were we waiting for? Did we go through the list of those attending in our heads and were insulted by the fact that none of them seemed important to us? Did we check how many celebrities were on the list? Were we just as pathetic as collectors who only ever mention the big hitters if asked what they collect? Although they were asked not "who", but "what". The very persona of an artist is at risk during exhibition previews, which is why these events are so tough on them. I had myself already published on the subject. And now here I was, exposing myself to the stress without even having an artistic oeuvre to my name. I put my behavior as a consumer up for public debate and in passing betray my friends. No wonder that such a maneuver causes stress. So much for a cultivated conversation in a leisurely atmosphere. Given the great inner tension I felt, irrespective of their actual content or the speaker's intentions, comments by guests inevitably seemed to be attacks.

Objectifying passion invariably fails

Ignorant questions, I feel, and yet I myself behave like a vacuous idiot and in paranoid-regressive fashion simply try and highlight prestige data via the art on display, instead of finding words for why this or that piece means something to me. My preoccupation with art defines my life. The pieces carefully chosen for the occasion are personally precious to me. I bitterly accuse myself of not being able to enthuse about artists, of feeling wooden when explaining an emotional attachment, as would essentially be expected of me in the situation. So here I am, betraying not only my friends but also art by hiding behind dry facts. When I notice that my gestures are freezing in place, I admonish myself to be more honest: "Simply say that it is love." In my head, I turn the matter now this way, now that: The benefit of a preoccupation with art is that there's always a bit left over that is pure passion. Art makes you happy.

Art is like falling in love at a flash.

Surely that is what makes collectors rich: more emotions. When traveling as a child, be it on holiday or to boarding school, I always had to bid farewell to a group of dolls and cuddly toys. On each occasion, my mother laughed at me and tended to narrate the occurrence to large groups of friends by way of amusement, even without there being cause to do so, and she loved to repeat the story. I myself feel just as embittered and unjust when I listen to myself describing the works on show. By reeling off knowledge, I betray that tender romantic bond, the passion for these works. As if in an auction catalog, a heroine in my life gets reduced to the status of being "born in a small town, died in another small town." In between an art piece that doesn't interest me in the slightest and where I do not even know the person who it is named after. Objectifying passion in this way must invariably fail. Collecting art and placing oneself in the service of a private collection are both highly personal acts. Are we capable of expressing and conveying strong emotions, and is an exhibition preview a good place to do so? A canonical one – most definitely not. How do others manage it? I immediately took a closer look at others in the market. It seemed to me as if the more relaxed guided tours of other private collections in rooms of their own had been those that took place in the absence of the collectors themselves. Should we perhaps follow suit and professionalize the museum by having it run by mercenaries? Did we need that distance to protect our privacy? Wasn't this again marred by some intrinsic pseudo-feudal view of things? Is it appropriate to act like the royals in Balmoral? – Guided tours only when the family is away, red velvet cords cordoning off certain areas. No, we needed to find a way forwards, we needed to make a change that was

Elisabeth von Samsonow
BABY, Performance
Photo: Maximilian Brucker → 180

less foolish and funny. The way things were unfolding in our house erased any sense of wishing to profess what our interests were, let alone be courageous. Because while I was busy wrestling with my inner self, something in the outside world inevitably happened that brought me back to earth. In the appropriate moment, the guests always acted inappropriately such that any romantic statement on what you yourself liked would have seemed insane. Things always unraveled quite mundanely. We had not foreseen that the guests in a private home always act as if they were attending a family member's housewarming, in other words mercilessly, the way one regularly only talks about people with whom one is related or of whom one assumes, despite their being in earshot, that they do not possess ears. The contents of the house, the garden, the neighborhood, even the shops in the vicinity, or the proximity to the airport (airplane thunder… but a practical location, of course) were discussed in our presence. Much later, when we had decided
to sell the house, these conversations were repeated in a 1
bizarre manner and at a point when we were inwardly at a long remove from anything and everything relating to the property. When people came to view the house, we walked round with them as if we were ourselves strangers to it and realized that the house's function was anything but clear. Absolutely no one who viewed it was able to imagine what a private museum was supposed to be. Hardly a surprise, then, that I had felt so confused.

Running the museum did not fulfill our expectation of sparking a permanent discourse, hosting a productive salon. The house was evidence of a plan that did not work in practice. We identified its fragmentary nature as being a central shortcoming in the project. Nothing ever got spun through to the end. The thread was forever breaking before we got there. We could not find a format that satisfied us enduringly. We looked forward to a specific date, everything was well prepared, and we felt we had a masterful command of the collection, and yet some detail, some figure, some title, was always not at hand. That never happened otherwise. If, on normal workdays, I walked past a picture, I had the feeling of being superbly informed about what was hanging there on the wall. Not that that's anything special. All collectors basically are masters of what I call the collector's quartet. You show off with ten Cindy Shermans versus one figurative Gerhard Richter. The complete set of Blinky Palermo prints outdoes any Alex Katz. Yet when you walk round the museum, specific detailed questions on this or that work have clearly been so overlooked that I cannot answer them. There is no point of reference. Actually, all of this is of no consequence, or so I tell myself in an effort to stay calm. No, I am not starting to suffer from dementia, but it's like going for a meal with someone you have just fallen in love with. You want to be liked; you want to lap up everything said solely in order to hear something that suggests your love is requited. There's a great risk of bewildering disappointment. You distrust things where you should really be open-minded, and you're babbling away when it would be better to keep your mouth shut; and the best things to say do not occur to you until you are unloading the dishwasher a few hours after the last guest has left or, as regards the first date, when everyone involved is at home alone in their beds. And what also prompts an uneasy feeling is the thought that some of those who ostensibly arrive in order to view art are in fact only seeking an excuse to add something. The offers by artists and gallerists are so rough-and-tumble, so in-your-face, that there is no scope for even appreciating the skillful dealers among them. No one wants to be the walking-talking wallet, and at the same time the collection is forever being rated in terms of: How much further potential is there to sell something? A nice evening with a gallerist, or in different social circumstances that for many years were informal, is now suddenly formal. What's happened here? Just like the collection visits in the past. You rate one another, you try and stand out from the crowd, now and then your mood crashes or you feel dissected and exposed.

Sometimes, I quite spontaneously combust, find the person I am talking to delightful, and imagine this could be the start of a friendship. Yet irrespective of whether we part agreeing to meet and go into things in depth or not, it somehow never happens, and the friendship is a non-starter. And should you meet again in some art context by coincidence, then you can't remember the name or topics discussed so ardently. Everything blurs. Yet the sense of unease remains. With the pandemic, our radius for movement was reduced; there was no thinking of receptions and openings. The museum followed Snow White into a deep sleep. We beat a retreat to Vienna and intended to eventually part company with the museum.

Can you readily market a castle in the air?

The idea of actually putting the house on the market sounded liberating. The marketing itself then had immense additional potential for frustration. Initially, various real estate agents were all enthusiastic, and wild were the fantasies about what the rooms could be turned into (i.e., who would buy them). The professional art storage depot in the basement was explored in terms of an alternative use: home movie theater, garage, DIY den, S&M studio – there was a bit of everything for everyone. In the case of the house, things proceeded just the way I knew from my work in commercial galleries – men got all fired up and women then put a dampener on things. Men loved the white cube; put off, the women complained that it was uncomfortable. The estate agents tried it with home-staging. Plans were drawn with lots of green planters in the house. The ground floor would be divided up into the individually useful rooms with clear functions. I stood straight and let my hands hang leisurely at my sides. I have frequently heard people using an attribute for me and adding an “actually”. Now the house suffered the same fate. In the process of separating from it, I made my peace with it because I identified with the protracted lack of understanding for it. As a building, it was not unsettling enough to silence all amateurish architectural criticism. And it was “designer” enough, not a Zaha Hadid work, as to prompt a trenchant description. Not Brutalist, not screaming for attention, but nevertheless strange, impossible to miss, and it seemed to have landed like a UFO in a district of town that boasted fences and garden gates. In other instances, it is I who am always the UFO, the strange creature who is “actually beautiful”. In my case, I lack the skin color and dark eyeliner, while the house lacked, or so the soon received opinion, two garages and a space for a large BBQ. How could I for so long have overlooked how similar the two of us were? What was special about us, designed so thoughtfully and staged, was now supposed to be a flaw. I apologized to the house and wished that it would find someone who would love its advantages in some eccentric way or other. Let it be the home to great happiness. Surely something had to be possible in these high, bright rooms in which so much of my husband’s longings had been cast in concrete, something that I could not really flesh out. Because surely, so much emotion could not simply disappear. Or so I hoped. Possible buyers emerged, my hopes started to wobble, but my unflagging optimism steamrollered my damning judgment of these individuals who wandered around the house blabbering and ostensibly thinking out loud. Most potential buyers thought I was an artist. And I was treated accordingly as a tender, decidedly crazy art producer. At times, I received looks such as those reserved normally for seven-year-olds spotting a “small person” for the first time at a fair. Now this was slightly damaging for the planned deal, as I was unable to play down my expertise as regards smart facilities technology, since the assumption was that I had no idea about the real world and had my head in the clouds. I praised myself for not feeling the impulse to state what my formal profession was, and instead accepted the odd opinion of my person with humor and even as an inverted compliment. After all, there were some interested parties who thought the property, both inside and out, was entirely of my own making. Sculptures and bronzes, virtuosity at the easel and brilliance with the graffiti spray-can, with the camera, making prints, devising installations. From there, it was a small step to congratulating me on my clothing, which they thought I had made myself. In future, we'd simply let the estate agent do the talking and be consciously absent.

Litigation against the social signifi- cance of your own actions doesn't work

I was happy to learn on the fly. So, the "artist" was not a buy-triggering point. I immediately attempted to profit from this and establish where I was vulnerable. I needed to transfer the feeling of "not-being-the-one-meant". Then I would be less prone to injury in other regards. There were clear areas to explore here. The gorilla in the room was forever cited as the explanation of why my husband and I were a couple. The responses to my being hitched to my husband were at times truly vicious, specifically among those who had known him during his marriage to his now deceased first wife – and among friends and admirers the reaction was strangely harsh. I was evidently not to be wounded by insinuations that we had known each other for ages beforehand and he had possibly kept me hidden away as a substitute family. That was something I had easily survived unscathed. The accusation that I had married him for his money I countered with the objection

that he had married me because I would be so useful. The notion that ours was an arranged marriage was thoroughly positive to my mind, since if you arrange a marriage, it means that third parties have decided that the two persons objectively fit well. I treated the repeated praise heaped on my husband's deceased first wife as a compliment, to which I replied: "So he's always had great women at his side." I went along with things only as far as my tolerance permitted. The one or other person I therefore simply deleted from the mailing list. Sometimes, in fact, my courage was exhausted and my sense of honor hard-hit. Lawyers say that it is impossible to litigate against your own actions for not being socially adequate. If you drive too fast, pay the fine. If you marry a blueprint, bear the consequences. I was thrown out of a fringe carnival association. That's fringe tolerance for you. They were so fringe that there was no formal procedure for throwing me out. I was simply turfed out. And that again taught me something. Years ago, a sociologist
1 reminded me of the decisive structure of things: Secretaries introduce an unplanned level of decision-making into companies and assume management functions. I was that secretary now and again. My son Konrad would say: "You can tell that at confession." Honorable it certainly was not, but a healthy act of emotional hygiene. Usually, however, I left my vizor up and was dismayed. For these were all well-educated, cultured people interested in art, and, completely at odds with their lives, at least to my mind, they sharply rejected the tie to a widower, in other words a single man, and treated me such that I invariably had to feel I was a mixture of consolation prize and emergency stopgap. They were forever emphasizing that the relationship purportedly lacked any prospects. Without asking for such, I was given any amount of advice on demographics: It would last ten years at least! Moreover: What, after all, could we do together? Setting up the company, family, house, collection; in all the areas touched on, there was no space for me and there was no potential for developing together. Over time, I became completely oblivious to the fact that people who

doubtless considered themselves liberal and tolerant came up with such nonsense. Initially I tried to explain that men do not feel their age at over 55, and accordingly, if "they are back on the market", seek companions who are younger than they are. And I was not that far off 55. Conversely, I asked the question of what those providing such unsolicited marital advice themselves imagined. What would have been the socially adequate alternative? If my husband said it had been clear to him that he would not stay single, then sporadically the response was, well they hadn't imagined it would go this way; instead perhaps an older woman, each person keeping their own apartment, weekend art trips, or the like. Proposing that as the suitable solution for an outstanding entrepreneur who loves life and doesn't want to be alone for one second sounds a little like: If these are your friends, who needs enemies? Although I have a quick tongue, I kept my reply to the matter of there only being ten years to myself: "Ten years of marriage, that's pretty damn long if you ask me." That was thus the point when my time as a student stood me in good stead. Initially my husband castigated me for having led a "hedonistic" life, and thus took the same line as one of my clients who objected that I always took the easy path. Over time, he learned to appreciate that I am not living out some father complex and am not inconstant, but free. Essentially, I had no real idea what these people were talking about. I heard the words being spoken, I saw how I was the subject of deliberations, but once again, evidently, I was not the person who was meant. Instead of possibly fretting at how short our time together might possibly be, I preferred to fill it with life.

Don’t ever say no to a last order

If you intend to spend the remainder of life with a person and that remainder may more probably be shorter than in other constellations, then every day is like “last orders” in the pub. Did I ever remain quiet when last orders were called? Of course not. I was swift of foot and the direction required was clear. Thanks to my lotus effect, bizarre occurrences did not serve to slow me down. For example: In light of my pending marriage, my mother pointed out to me that in the event of death “Herr Schmidt will be buried next to his wife,” intending in this way to make it clear to me that my marriage would only be window-dressing. In that instance, I did not hold my tongue but quick-wittedly retorted that burial duty was a legal consequence of marriage. Thus, I would have him buried wherever I so chose. I then purchased a grave in the “millionaire’s avenue” in Melaten, Cologne’s central cemetery, and took my life into my own hands. The house had to be sold. Why was it taking so long? What could I, for my part, do in order to speed up the sales process? Identically to the conversion of my personal wardrobe, it soon became clear to me that we could not go on explaining we were giving up the house because we were relinquishing the private museum. And I was not guessing, as I had tried the proposition out and the person looked at me as if I had said we were selling up because the house was haunted. What explanation could there be for us giving up the museum that was not completely wrong, but which outsiders would readily understand? We took as our example people who, for all manner of reasons, don’t pursue a career and use the pretense of the children. At one level that was wrong, as the kids liked the house. No one else lived in a detached house with a personal elevator in which there was always a chair. The house served their needs superbly. Jakob was of the opinion that the house had far more hiding holes than any other. They praised its spaciousness: “I can ride my scooter indoors and wheel in the table-tennis table if it rains.” On School Hikes Day the children invited the whole class round, and for their first communion over 60 guests sat at one long table. Our favorite brewery, Früh am Dom, came by with all the staff required to prepare schnitzel for all and sundry. At the refectory table in the library, the meal was prepared on innumerable small plates. The Vienna Boys Choir arrived in their touring bus and stayed a while to have fun in the garden and to “chill out”. I was relieved that the children let us go ahead with the sale, even though they liked the place. We therefore explained our leaving Cologne with the fact that the children were both members of said Vienna Boys Choir and we wanted to be close to them there. Everyone understood that. That all members of the choir are obliged to attend boarding school, even those boys who live just round the corner, was something we simply neglected to mention. It’s best to only make a mistake once. When we mentioned that the children would be in boarding school, something that for me was completely normal, we were immediately suspected of getting them out of the way. In short, anyone exiting their familiar sociological biotope needs to endure uncertainty. I am clearly terribly naïve, as I was unable to preempt anything; with each step, new critical issues arose that left me speechless and stress-tested my quick wit, on which I could otherwise always rely. In any Debrett’s, you’ll read that certain topics are not fit for small talk. Oozing eczema, war, salaries, the sex life of the person you are talking to, religion. I was thus honestly astonished then when I provoked people merely by saying I would not attend Sunday matinee because then I would be competing with High Mass. Children who want to sing in a famous choir were the result of our own exaggerated ambition. Irresponsible, exposing them in boarding school to criminal acts against sexual self-determination. As if all that were written in stone. And we were accused of not being able to manage our money, as we idiots paid church tax, however customary that may be in Germany. If I say that I don't let individuals spoil my fundamentally excellent relationship with Jesus, I get told that I am mad. There was a time when I defiantly insisted my persistently effusive good mood was the product of my strictly nurtured, child-like faith. To no avail. I realized the need to adapt when it came to my clothes, and I also get it with Jesus. Nothing has changed whatsoever since the matter of the school milk. If I'm too far removed from the others' mindset, then I don't reveal my hand. At the same time, I remain optimistic and simply wait until we get so familiar that there comes a point when we can possibly talk about it after all. Sometimes there are moments when suddenly everything falls into place. After we had been married for about a year, I heard my husband say on the phone, "No, the Friends of Museum XYZ could not visit". Of course, he continued to whomever was at the other end, these friends were important, an important association, of course, but they were not "our" friends. The load that fell off my mind was so great that the district shook: "Someone is making certain I am not in the firing line – what a stroke of good fortune that I married him."

Standalone failures

We still had to deal with the museum and the association of friends that went with it. Because collectors can sustain narcissistic injuries without a museum of their own, too. The entire loans segment is also a good breeding ground for severe wounds to be inflicted. An example: We supply high-res reproductions, we assume the insurance for the loan, I offer to check the catalog before it goes to print. All of that is rejected, as the museum staff are all pros; and then there's the issue of scholarly freedom, or so I am told from on high. All of which spells: Our image is printed upside down in the printed version of the catalog. Since there is a line of script in the image, to my mind the catastrophic mistake is apparent to anyone. The artist rings up, the gallery rings up, "Dearest, what on earth is going on?" I was really angry. At least I managed to dream up an elegant statement: "I only very reluctantly do not gainsay the standalone failures of others." Namely, of precisely those who should have heaped ashes on their heads before me but instead obliviously commented: "Oops, sorry, see you at the fundraising-dinner. Till then." I don't like the entire thrust of this. My dedication to specific artistic positions, my joy in experiencing artworks and to be able to go for a walk in them as if in the eyes of a loved one sitting opposite me, and at the same time being useful on behalf of the art in the context of the collection – all of that I very enthusiastically embraced, and possibly with a streak of innocence. I wanted to preserve that feeling and not to have to defend it. I don't want to have to argue and fight stridently for this tender bond. No one asks you why you love your children or your dog. There are relationships about which no one dares pose really trenchant questions. At any rate, not as regards children or the dog. All other tender bonds are evidently exposed to leveling, to scorn, and a tribunal. Is it too much to ask to let something live without having to discuss it, without having to call for what is deemed “respect” in the school yard, and in my life, somewhat old-schoolish, as “decency, good behavior, and manners”? Crazy! Heterosexual family fathers who spend the weekend behind their BBQs, tax officers and forwarding agents, all of them send text messages with little hearts and call you “dear” or “darling”, but talking about love is supposed to nevertheless be such an awkward matter? I once termed collecting art “love for sale”. A useful positioning? Or is consumerism even harder to explain and at times even embarrassing? I sense that fleeing into “objectivity” is perhaps a productive form of self-protection. Will I soon also start talking in platitudes like “giving something back to society, gratitude, social responsibility”? Aren’t these all clever ciphers to avoid having to say what Kaiser Franz put this way: “No one knows how much I loved this woman.”

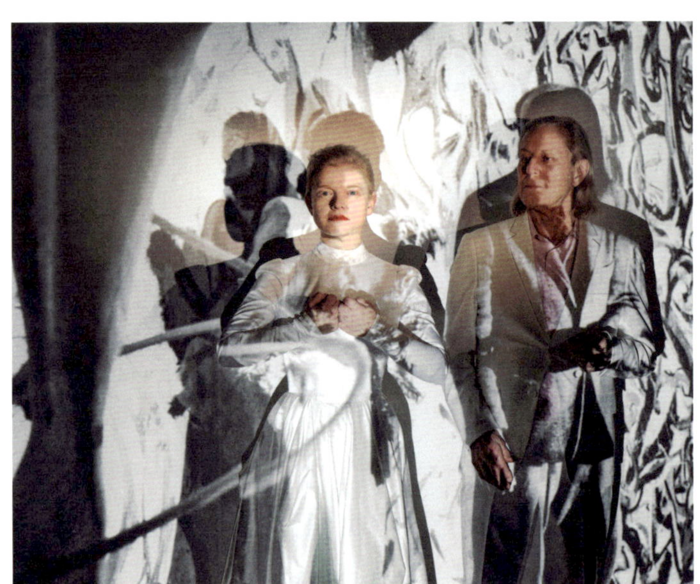

Clegg & Guttmann: PROJECTION PORTRAIT
(PEGGY GUGGENHEIM AND MAX ERNST)

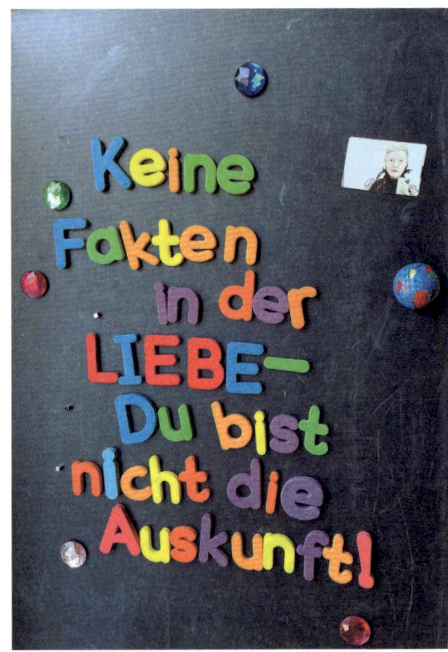

No facts in LOVE –
You're not the Information Desk!

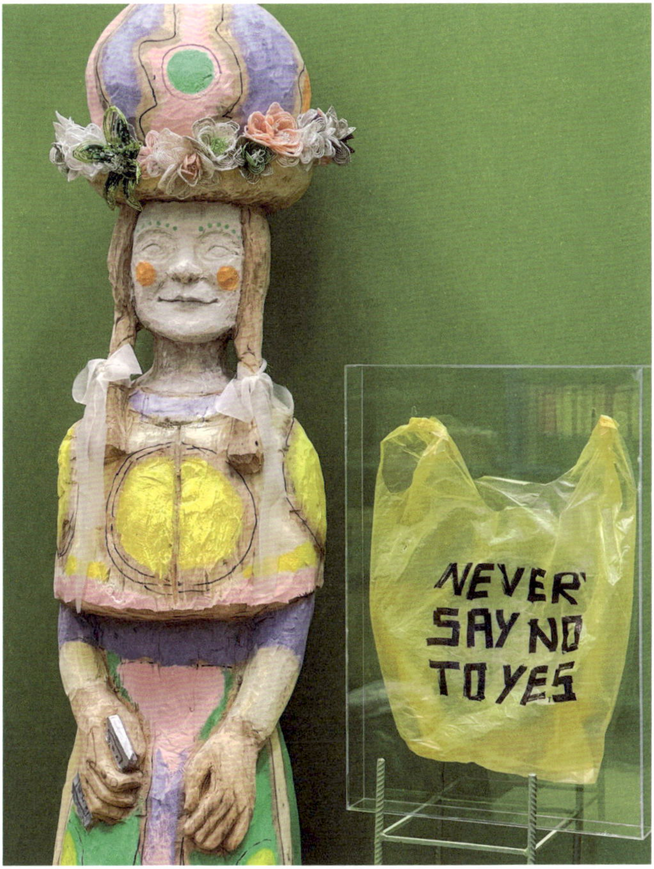

Elisabeth von Samsonow SASA
Driton Selmani NEVER SAY NO TO YES

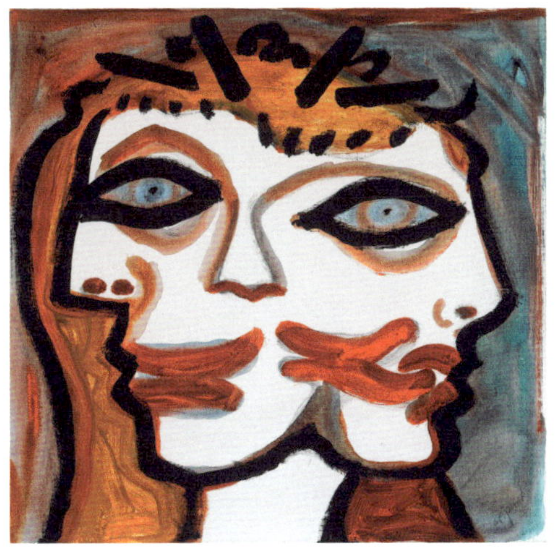

A. R. Penck SASA

1

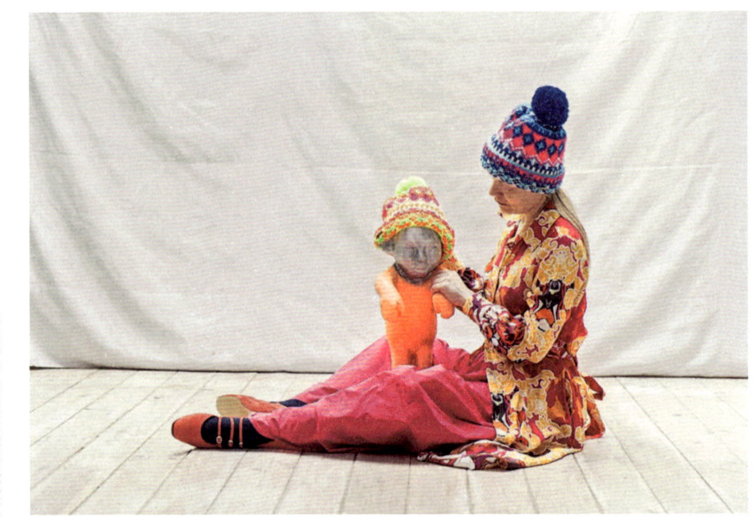

Elisabeth von Samsonow BABY, Performance
Photo: Maximilian Brucker

Dear painter, come play with me

We bade farewell to the concept of the semi-public home for a collection. As after a severe illness (to relate it to my personal experience) following final-year exams, the pressure simply fell away. The daughter of friends said, after a really nasty infection: “Right, I’m done now with being ill.” I was done with the museum. We were done with it. Healed, appeased, and strengthened. Putting the private collection on public display has proved to be a shallow promise despite the resources (not that we had really budgeted them) available to it. Money doesn’t always buy you goals. It did us so much good to be able to let the whole thing be without regret or a gnashing of teeth. What, looking back, was the reason why it was the wrong path for us to take? The pressure that one ostensibly exerts on oneself in order to have gotten a suitable exhibition hung and ready on time because some museum’s association of friends is dropping by, because the curator of some museum has announced a visit as s/he is on the lookout for loans, because the trade-fair circus has come to town? No. Walking the tightrope between the needs associated with private life and the requirements of a public building was not painful, paralyzing, or inhibiting. For we are energetic folk and felt in our own unconventional manner that we were capable of doing things. In fact, over time we became really good at living in the house and hosting larger events on the spur of the moment.

Just because I can doesn't mean I have to

One of the largest lessons learned down through decades of work, however, is definitely that just because I can do something doesn't mean I have to. We both no longer wanted to, because it led to a lull in our personal engagement with art. Our conversations increasingly seemed to be held through a filter, as if brought to a halt by some strange case of stage fright. The pandemic granted us this insight and helped drive the change process. The entire core family increasingly felt that the period with no exhibition openings (either of our own or elsewhere), with no events, art fairs, or fundraising dinners, and also without school for the kids or art-related travel, was a boon, a bubble of happiness. Possibly, we were also suffering from social burnout. Because we were indeed exhausted by all the dysfunctional encounters associated with hosting exhibitions and only managed to earth ourselves thanks to the legally imposed standstill and the lack of undertakings. The external conditions were ripe for this: No one fell seriously ill; we didn't take an economic hit. We of course noticed how the world around us had come unstuck. We were concerned about what was happening out there, but without suffering directly. Perhaps one can call it a gift for happiness, the ability to let different, countervailing worlds exist next to each other. We mourned acquaintances who died and felt sorry for those who had to suffer at various levels. At the same time, our domestic tableau unfolded before us and in the course of that year really blossomed instead of becoming a habit or petering out. We were carefree and unconcerned. There was no space to worry that we might miss something. It was very clear we wouldn't miss anything. Even with my great routine in working from home, I had no difficulty formulating one and the same letter declining invitations; sometimes it did hurt a bit after all, turning someone down as per usual. Staying at home while out in the world elaborately curated exhibitions were taking place always had a bit of laziness, disinterest, immodesty, and playing truant about it. Moreover, I actually like saying “Yes”, we talked about this. During the pandemic, staying at home was more than socially adequate behavior, and I no longer had to justify it to myself or excuse myself for being stubborn. Suddenly, it was exemplary behavior to avoid social contact, as you could protect yourself and others from illness. Against this backdrop, my ability to live in the here and now and make something of what was at hand instead of hoping for inspiration from the outside really came into its own. Life with the children and two other boys from the choir, who were semi-stranded at our place and were halfway extended family, was quite literally wonderful. Full of wonders. So much for the ostensible greater social stress of being with four teenagers! The rare opportunity to watch these youths up close, all four full of experiences and well versed with the ways of the world from their times traveling with the touring section of the Vienna Boys Choir was something I lapped up. My husband still speaks (and not only seeing things through the dreamy spectacles of retrospection) of it having been “the greatest time ever”, and indeed said the same back in the acute moments of the lockdowns and the restricted scope they brought with them. For me, everyday life in this leisurely grouping felt like my childhood before I went to school or like the great flat-shares, specifically outside of term-time. Our daily rhythm was not dictated by the outside world, and instead of drying up we casually flourished. Many things lent themselves to being used creatively. We were a community that did not know boredom or despair, and instead formed a lively adventure society. Instead of getting trapped in lethargy as life had been scaled back a gear or two, we acted. We told one another about our worlds, school, profession, travels, and developed utopias, such as how school could be, who should shape school life,

Angela Glajcar
DREAMCATCHER - TRAUMFÄNGER → 216

and how school could be individualized. Sometimes we also got caught up intensively in quite mundane topics. At some point we found ourselves talking about rent and started to try and fathom it all out. All the different things relating to renting an apartment in a tenement block in Dresden served as the basis for days exploring the subject. How to calculate the rent, how to market an apartment to let, what does an estate agent actually do, what is a deposit, how much do you need to earn to be able to afford an apartment that costs 1,000 Euros net, what is a notary who does not also act as a lawyer? In this light, we were already living the utopia of a school that interlinked academic topics with their practical application. In the final analysis, for us, all the lockdowns amounted to a school project. Because we consciously watched award-winning movies and extensively discussed historical contexts. We took turns cooking and brought a variety of ideas to bear on what the menu should hinge on: national cuisine, avoiding waste, in keeping with the season, or all of one and the same color. We agreed to meet for joint undertakings inside the house, we sang to one another, we read out loud, dreamed, and slept, and woke up whenever it best suited us and fitted life in our little community.

Every child knows what makes you happy

The knowledge that humans are pack animals and that life in a group with others makes you happy if you can live a balance between closeness and distance is neither new nor surprising. Having to live exclusively over a longer period of time in the “pack” and to live with the space we had available was as if we had been transformed into an installation by Angela Glajcar: lightness and gravity, views inwards, view through things, attraction and tension, calm and inner agitation, warmth and muted sounds, sharply torn edges, ruptures. Looking back, all these details form an overall sculpture that stands there laconically like a psychological profile while also inviting you to enter and inhabit it. We adults considered our personal psychological profiles to be that of outstanding entrepreneurs. We can aspire and fight. What makes us truly satisfied is the absence of that. Not because we don't want to be entrepreneurial, but because we know we can do it and only fight where it makes entrepreneurial sense. Alongside the sharp torn edges and the clear lines, to remain with the metaphor of an Angela Glajcar piece, we emphasize the share played by lightness, by floating. The paper volumes in her expansive works give rise to worlds that are like walking through snow. Everything is light and soft and dampened, enchanting thanks to the modulated white, while also having clearer contours itself. The "spatial concept", to remain with the metaphor of the feeling of life described as an art installation, made lines of sight possible that we now had the leisure to explore. We sounded out doctrines to gauge their role and utility in our life. Exploring my own emotions as regards when exactly art felt best, I found out that I am most fruitfully close to the individual works if I create collages in my thought. The motto set for my husband's collection was "Collect in order to curate". That seemed a little hifalutin to me, but over time this sense of self-empowerment has ceased to be completely foreign to me. Because I feel good when I am inwardly curating and comparing art, associating and linking substantive aspects and creative forms to one another, superimposing them along the way. The question as to how to make these processes visible to the outside world and share them was something I could not initially answer. During the pandemic there were no exhibitions, and hangings in the rooms we inhabited no longer needed to be commented on as if they were some special curatorial achievements. Nevertheless, this insight into my inner collaging had practical consequences. I thus consciously for a while desisted from any busy work in the storage room.

Collector on duty

Because creating order and repeatedly sorting things anew as a way of approaching an art collection increasingly seemed to me to be a secondary aspect to my focus on our collection. The frequency of the physical engagement with the collection was something I no longer needed as proof to the outside world that I took the collection seriously. I took the matter seriously and I did not need to spend billable hours in the storage room. I was not a salaried staff member on duty in the collection. How, then, to behave as a collector on duty? Ordering in the manner of coin or stamp collectors seemed to me to be a very reductive, not to say anally compulsive, manner of engaging with the collection on a daily basis. To that extent, I already had in my head the butterfly that was about to have a pin stuck through it. How could I engage with art, specifically the art I had taken on, that my husband had brought with him into the marriage, in such a way that it brought a spring to my step? The method of approaching art by casting litigable results in abundantly accurate Excel charts is one way. Gaining an overview of things when taking on a collection lays the foundations for all else. Yet the less I had to prove to myself that I was serious, the more an inner bond could evolve. I was not alone in searching for new ways to engage with our art holdings, which were meanwhile well sorted and catalogued. The busy-bee diligence of the early years had not only had a beneficial effect for me. My husband said that he had the feeling that he had been collecting for decades, in order now, with my appearance on the scene, to be able to talk about it in peace and quiet and in that way engage properly with the collection for the first time. He had basically stocked up in advance.

Living from the stocks

For me, the idea of "stocks" set a lot in motion. "Setting up stocks" was a procedure I was clearly familiar with from childhood. The pantry in my childhood had not depended on going shopping each day. In my family's cellars, sausages and hams hung from the ceiling and preserved fruit lined the shelves; the potato crates that smelled so profoundly of earth apparently never grew empty, and earthen tubs of sauerkraut were sealed tight with wooden lids held down by large stones. Golden cans of sausage rose up in towers, and the narrower shelves were home to the stocks of apples, nuts, and pears. Each time I visited my Aunty Waltraud, I inspected the huge glass jar next to the cucumbers that cuddled up in their little jars with the red rubber rings like whelps in a doggie basket. The big jar – and it was as big as the neighbors' aquarium – housed a special delicacy, namely beetroot cut in thin slices. Using a long wooden spoon, sometimes a small portion was extracted from it specially for me. Just as in the country they say that you need to stock up during the summer and fall, so, albeit unconsciously, I had prepared duly for the winter collector's blues. The stocks I had assembled were to be found between the covers of books. I started working up my diary entries and some of my publications as if they had been written by someone else. Despite my generally good memory, many of the entries and passages in articles were foreign to me. I had not forgotten them in the narrower sense, it was just that I was now reading them against a different backdrop. My world had changed significantly. In line with my fundamental optimism, I no longer worried that collectors were the others and thus the object of my thoughts; rather, it was suddenly all about me. The legal craft is embedded in me as deeply as the apples in the tart when fresh from the oven. I now wished to make pragmatic use of the perspective from the outside that was exhibited by my earlier jottings and publications. As if compiling a legal opinion, I assessed the individual character traits of collectors the way I had described them. What would my research lead to? I had always found thinking without worrying about what the results might be very satisfying, even at times when the possible result might not help me in the particular situation. In the process, I admonished myself to be merciful with myself. I had stated that, as regards collectors, one reason for engaging with art was to test their courage, meaning to test themselves in light of the real decisions to be made. Designing the collection as it was being assembled, and the involvement with art per se, were correspondingly often a boost to one's qualities as an entrepreneur. I therefore set about identifying topics that I could test my courage on. At what points would I need to overcome myself and should do just that?

Farewell collectior Darwinism

One major difficulty I needed to work on was the comfort zone in which I had taken refuge as regards art I had acquired myself. Hitherto, I had not defined myself as a collector. My art holdings had arisen, I thought, purely from my work. The art served as documentation, souvenir, and trophy rolled into one. This pleasant self-definition, which sidestepped having to state the free consumerist decision, now needed to shed its skin. It was a fairly massive leap, as two hurdles had to be overcome. First, I had to confess to myself that the art which had come to be in my possession and accompanied my life also rested in each instance on conscious decisions. Little of it had simply eventuated, for example as a gift. This first step was comparatively easy to take. It was harder when it came to my husband's collection. Because merely caring for and preserving the collection into which I had married in the role of manager and curator would mean evading the responsibility to myself to stand behind the selection of art in question. Once again, the art would simply have happened, as it were. The collection was not my job but was supposed to become my life. Showing little mercy to myself, I demanded of myself that I pin my colors to the mast and not only undertake correct supplementations or streamlining of the works, but also start to impress my own stamp on it. I succeeded. As regards art, I increasingly took clear choices. That cleared the path for us to undertake something jointly. After years of relative stagnation as regards the holdings, we started (in terms of my husband: once again) to buy art in a bigger way. Collecting is immodest, or so I had lectured in the past.

Portraits

Prior to moving from the art-market professional side of things to that of the collec-
9 tors, I had once already flirted with immodesty. Commissioning A. R. Penck to paint a portrait of me on canvas was anything but modest. The outstanding quality of the piece and the very famous artist helped prevent almost any possible painful criticism arising. I always ironically subverted my grandiose gesture. I find the idea of commissioning a portrait interesting for several reasons. In the play Doing Your Business, which I authored together with Hanspeter Horner, the pseudo-feudal gesture of the commissioned portrait is taken to the point of absurdity with a collection mentioned that consists solely of portraits of the collector. After all, strange things can happen in the search for a unique characteristic for a private collection. How far removed is the collection in which everything is in square formats (because the collectors' product, which generated the money for the collection, is square) from a gallery of ancestors with no ancestors? The collector intends to establish a dynasty. In the absence of other actors, only he is portrayed. Others will follow. Or so he imagines. In this way, in "Doing Your Business", a comedy,

A. R. Penck SASA → 179

collecting art is mocked as an attempt by the nouveau riche to makes themselves seem important. As a former cabaret artist, I am fully aware of how you go about making a joke: What you attack is the target. The fact that you can laugh about immodesty does not therefore mean it does not exist. On the contrary, the yearning to be a "big man" is a precondition for it. My customary manner of taking a scalpel to everything left no other rational conclusion possible. At the same time, engaging with art is of course precisely not just a rational matter. How often have I said or written that for me good art starts where the discourse stops? This is the very key to why it did me good to repeatedly agree to sit for artists. The test to anyone's courage of being completely exposed to the artist's eye is something I have successfully passed, and for me it is comparable to the collector's courage in professing his predilection for a particular artistic position. In large part, abandoning control of how you stage yourself and waiting to see what the person on the other side of the easel or camera sees and can use in me has always set something very precious in motion in me. If, when assessing art, I am confronted with statements such as "Why is that so expensive? The artist can't have spent more than ten minutes on it", I always try and explain things to my opposite in a way that can work. I don't bother with outlining the complex criteria for how value arises in art, taking this minute work on paper costing 20,000 Euros as an example, but reduce things to the most important factor driving value of them all, namely a piece's membership of an oeuvre as a whole: "It is precisely by purchasing this sheet cobbled together in a few minutes that you are locking into decades of professional experience. The way the famous surgeon does, although he only operates on you for less than an hour. He brings all his experience to bear in his work and in the fee he then charges." Taking part in a performance, or being incorporated into performative photography, conveys the same meaning to me in relation to myself. Working in theater, ballet, involvement in fashion – all of this is useful in that

moment when the camera is focused on me. All those experiences have to then be at hand, ready to be placed in the service of this, another person's work. And then things go well. Then it's no longer about me as a private person. Frequently, I am asked with reference to works where I served as the subject matter whether I think I am beautiful in them. That is once again a situation in which I do not really know where to start, because for me the question as to my own beauty in connection with a piece of art is wrong at so many different levels. Sitting as model means me, the private person, courageously exposing myself to an outside eye. In this context, courageous means to have an open heart, to leave my vizor up. Then, if things go well, I will find out something about myself that I didn't know before. If I want to be beautiful in my definition, then I retain control and take a reasonable selfie instead. In other words, sitting as a model is an unknown trip inwards; wanting to be beautiful is part of presenting yourself to the
1 outside world. The objective of both processes of creating images differs fundamentally. It's excellent if an artwork in which I am depicted highlights an aspect of me that even I can find attractive, too.

Double portrait

The thing got tricky when I received an enquiry from Clegg & Guttmann, as their portraits reflect the life of the person depicted. In other words, the focus is not on providing the surface for the artist's creative idea, but the person shown is meant to be a prime example for a stance or a sociological group and populate it like a kind of blueprint. Wanting to portray my husband and myself was thus an alarming prospect, just as it was flattering. What were we supposed to stand for? In the course of the preliminary exploratory conversations, it emerged that the artists' approach was something we both liked. Our concern said more about our fears than about

Clegg & Guttmann: PROJECTION PORTRAIT (PEGGY GUGGENHEIM AND MAX ERNST) → 178

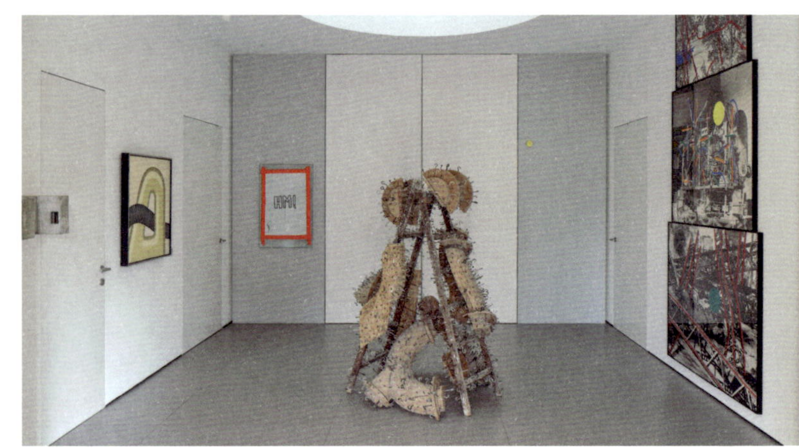

Cologne Museum: Oliver Czarnetta, Konrad Klapheck, Tobias Rehberger, Tony Cragg, Christian Frosch, John Baldessari, Photos: Sasa Fuis

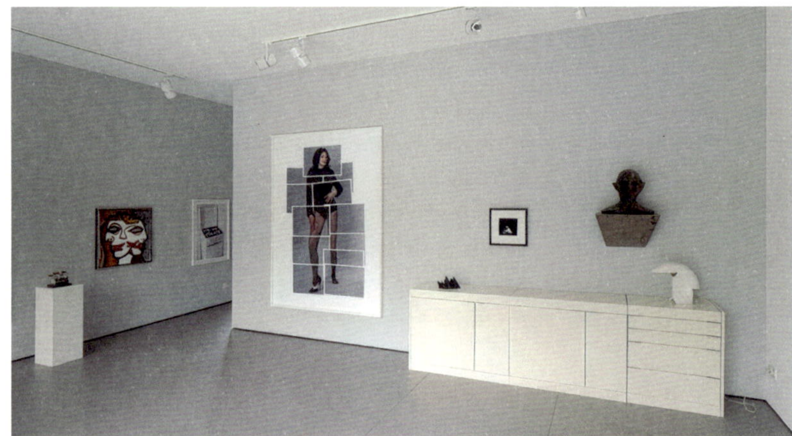

Rose Eken, A. R. Penck, Andreas Gursky, ULAY, Nan Hoover (2), Thomas Schütte

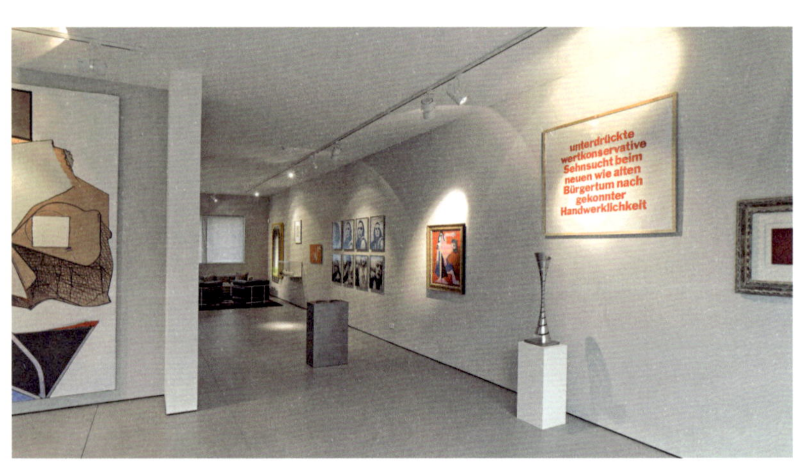

T. Scheibitz, T. Rehberger, R. Trockel (2), T. Dietz, J. Klauke, R. Trockel (Herd), E. L. Kirchner, T. Demand, M. Willing, F. E. Walther

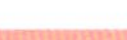

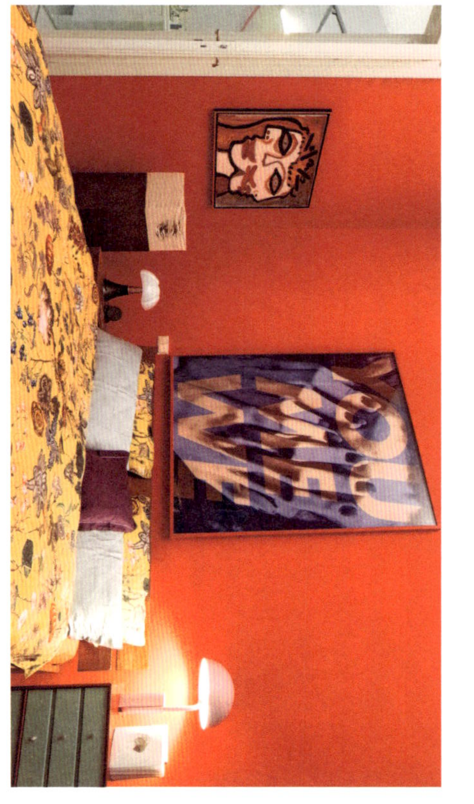

A. R. Penck, Angela Glajcar (2),
Barbara Kruger

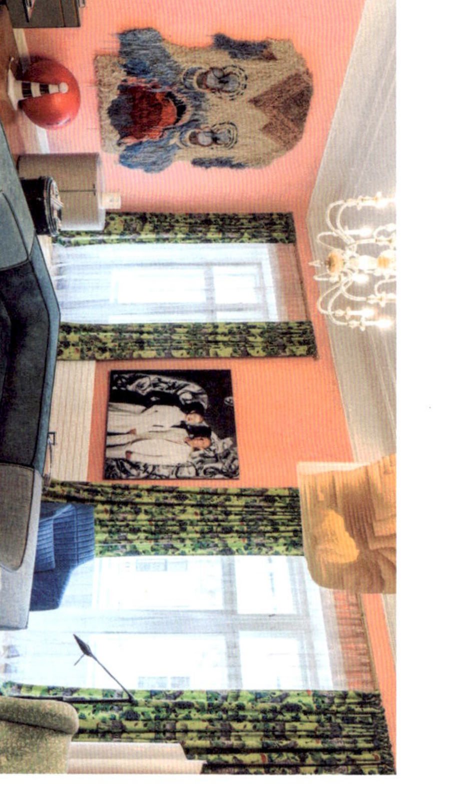

Caroline Achaintre, Angela Glajcar (2),
Clegg & Guttmann, Photos: Jürgen T. Sturany

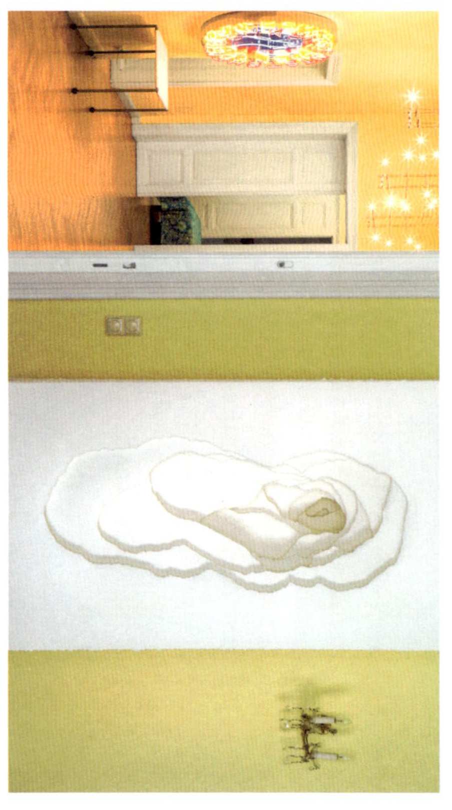

Vienna apartment: Ferdinand Kriwet,
Angela Glajcar, Photo: Werner Lieberknecht

what the artists were undertaking. Clegg & Guttmann said their objective was to portray a giant merger, a marriage of Titans. They were looking for an art market couple, not a collector couple in the narrower sense. In the final instance I was delighted, because the role I was to have I really liked, namely playing the part of Peggy Guggenheim. Her eccentric way of turning half a palazzo in a foreign city (the building had never been completed and was now dilapidated) into a vibrant, multifaceted place for art was my absolute ideal. The mixture of Max Ernst and Peggy Guggenheim as a couple to be represented by ourselves was an adventure that we could very much embrace. Even the preparations were exciting, such as the concern regarding my dress, which was to oscillate between an original dress worn by Peggy Guggenheim and my own style of clothing, while also providing enough white space for the projection of the original photo. Markus Spatzier took on the task, and both the dress and to my mind the later works were just right. My husband was, by then, worried as regards the actual dates of the photo shoots but, when push came to shove, liked his transformation, his displacement into the photos that arose. The entire project was very enriching for us, both together and individually. We benefited not just by becoming part of the artist duo's oeuvre, but above all, this journey on which we had embarked together did us a lot of good on the inside. After many years, and over and above the work on the project itself, these sittings for the double portrait sparked new and well-considered thoughts on how we would deal with the setting of this "marriage of Titans". Who wanted or could contribute something to it, and what could still be done over and above what we had already achieved? Instead of being cowed by the objections from the outside, with all their concerns as regards the timeline and substantive horizon of our marriage, for us the images manifested the fact that in our engagement with art, and probably in our time together, we stood firmly rooted in tradition(s), had role models and personal heroes. At the same time, we were able to see how special our situation was, even if it was not unique, and wanted to continue nurturing it together as originally as possible. One thing was clear: We explicitly wanted to be seen together. We had beforehand thought of and considered various things, tried them out, and now gradually hit great form together, for a joint public image. The visualization in the double portrait as two persons who, in the public perception, were not seen as a couple and rather each unto themselves had a liberating effect. There was no need for each to stick to his/her particular view or for us necessarily to do everything together, and yet it was all about art. We didn't want to hide behind a fabricated presumptuous duty to convert other people to art. We took ourselves and the collection seriously. To us, everything else seemed dishonorable.

Not getting a handle on things, but getting them going

Because anyone who maintains a large collection, with all the loans transactions and all the related matters, has to take it seriously. You don't fill art depots or the pages of a book casually and without reflecting on things. Is it not deeply human to gladly show something that you feel is precious to the outside world, and that the enjoyment is all the greater if you can share it with others? For me, some questions are not out of place and incomprehensible. If someone asked me why I wanted children, I found the question very strange, and it astonished me in an unpleasant way. Is it not human and somehow "normal" in the course of things to want to have children? For me, at any rate, a successful life entailed: bearing, supporting, nurturing relationships at all manner of levels, meaning a life in the pack, and not just with a small nuclear family as my reference system. Moreover, I really like it if everything is structured in such a way that I need not have any fears. I accordingly expect of myself that without putting up any inner resistance, I carefully and efficiently concern myself with such unsexy assets as old-age provisions and other profane matters. For me, that's part of a life with well-ordered stocks, and is perhaps even an important part of the foundations on which effusiveness and tranquility can flourish. All of it taken together, enjoying the stocks, effusiveness, and tranquility, only then comes into full effect and kindles happiness if they are not lived and enjoyed alone but together with others. The deeper we dug into ourselves, the more we realized that here lay the greatest common ground between us as a couple. Separated by different paths through life and by a generation, this was the point where there was very great overlap.

Love is no somethin limitec

If you have children, you don't love the third one less. Love is not something limited. It is only the aspect of whether you can raise them that seems to be as perfidious and limited in terms of your lifetime as is the production of insulin. Or so it seems to me. I thought my parents in one way or another were not strict enough with me, could not be bothered to keep a check on me, as I was the last-born child. I have not observed anything like this in myself, as with only two children I have not come up against the limits of my energy. In this context, less is again not more, and enjoying art in a small, exclusive circle of people does not necessarily promise me more enjoyment. My husband and I agreed on this. We did not want to be like the Lilliputians and have people stare at us like some strange species from the outside; no, we wanted to share the enjoyment. This meant in relation to art: We wanted to be seen. We wanted interaction and to share with others. It was clear to us that the wish to continue to be perceived by others rests on the desire to create a monument to ourselves. In the face of such reservations, we simply shrugged our shoulders inwardly and physically. My husband had already laid a lot of foundations and even built a museum for the collection. It other words, our commitment was clear: The collection had to endure. But how exactly? What shape could shared enjoyment take? How to create a setting in which enjoyment could evolve? Can enjoyment be planned? We of course went on the front foot. A hotel, a beautiful garden – those are likewise worlds of enjoyment, with the difference being that we were already familiar with those formats. In our case, strategic considerations entailed an equation with countless unknown variables. Would we simply move from the frying pan into the fire and come under immense pressure, albeit no longer from the museum but from the successor format? Would the uncertainty and the explorative search again go hand in hand with the stress of having to assert ourselves? Keeping an eye on the others in the peloton, or the market players, as the commercial pundits would put it, would, or so I recognized, lead straight back to social prestige neurosis, once again not being very kind to myself. I had established such a nice, comfortable life for myself. Was this then not all about positioning us in a completely opaque setting and considering how well positioned one was oneself? Were we fit enough to endure, or could we get fitter? If one can't evade collection Darwinism, given that attention is a limited asset, what does one do? I was able to feel on top of things and knowledgeable in my small and well-ordered environment. I could truly hear Jens Beckert lecturing on the loops that created significance in the art market. For me, what this meant was: Woe unto those who leave their comfortable beaten tracks. Irrespective of whether you start professionally in another museum or gallery, or inherit a collection, or, like me, step into it via marriage: No two loops are the same, and at any rate one part of the art world remains, one that is unknown, one where you know no one, or – and this can be far worse depending on your personality structure – no one knows you. These structures are the happy well-font of ice-cold water in the face. After decades of work, I had a little practice in not being triggered by the like. And now "all" I had to do was transpose this onto the collection. I started actively formulating new principles and establishing defense mechanisms. Instead of being insulted that the art offerings manifestly did not correspond to what we considered our theme to be, it was worth identifying that it was only our own vanity that was affected. Several things helped in this regard. First, why relate the fact that others don't read or listen back to my own person? And second, what can I do differently so that others stop thinking their goods would fit us? Finally, why do I ask myself such adolescent questions and get worked up? We could talk to each other like adults and simply say: You, yes you, do you have any idea what we're doing here? If testing it as an inner monolog didn't work, then I'd have to resort to the old boarding-school adage and observe: Perhaps it won't be to my detriment if I honestly help someone else understand what we're doing here and answer factually. Not be miffed, not be preachy, and instead invite and encourage? Then I will at least have tried my best. At any rate, it was worth always remembering the principle about how to engage with art and the constant degradations in the art market: "We are not nothing, and we don't need to save." The regular laws of an opaque market cannot be controlled. You can't get a handle on any of it. So, the objective can at best be to go with the flow. The hardest part is probably accepting chance: whom you encounter in the course of things and how ready that person is to listen at that particular moment in time. Thus, a fairly brief conversation with Lothar Baumgarten that arose by chance fundamentally shaped how I grasped the interior design of living spaces. Half an hour with Lothar Baumgarten put ground under my feet. Other encounters made no impression.

It is not fruitful to emphasize trivial moments that are of no consequence. Anyone who is treated throughout life as an elf (or, optionally, an angel, a fairy, or Pretzel Goddess) will now or then encounter a miracle. Of that I was firmly convinced.

A miracle always intervenes

And there it was, the miracle. In the form of being offered a property. The neighbor who helped with the search called it “a writing bureau for the beautiful woman”. Writing was one goal. Since all sorts of other things would be negotiated here, work performed of a commercial nature (family office, studio management for Angela Glajcar), I soon had a name for it: my comptoir. Even the address was incredible. Because Schmerlingplatz is one of the venues in Heimito von Doderer’s novel “The Demons”, where word has it that you only need to “carve out as large an area as possible in which chance can operate” in your favor (Heimito von Doderer, THE DEMONS, vol. 1, tr. R. & C. Winston [Knopf: New York, 1961], p. 384). And there the place stood before me, and I immediately fell in love with it. Schmerlingplatz 2. A ground floor store to the right of the entrance. Its two large arches lay closed behind wooden shutters that had been down for years. One arch is a window, the other meant for a double-door. That became visible once, with much patience and force, the blinds were cranked open. The interior was dark, run down, clammy cold. The elegant lady who was meant to show me round the place was embarrassed at having to present such a “poky hole”. The place found, only two doors down from our apartment in Vienna, immediately fired my imagination, which I therefore likewise had to reel in. I saw myself, a mixture of Peggy Guggenheim and Pippi Longstocking, sitting in these rooms. In furs and with elven clothes, spectacles with glittering stones, or a diadem in my hair. That is how I would sit, doll-like, in the display window, writing, pondering, and doing business. On the sidewalk in front of the store, I would sit on small chairs and talk with people, and we would gaze at the trees on Schmerlingplatz and undress passers-by with our eyes and/or engage them in conversation, depending… I even went so far as to find the miracle a custom-fit. Neither vast nor small, 125 square meters, window, door. And airy. How often are miracles so practical? For me, of course, much derived from the idiosyncrasies of this enchanted beauty. The place where my desk would stand, directly opposite the window, and with my back to the stairs leading down to the cellar (which didn't yet exist). A huge Angela Glajcar installation would hang above me, I would sit and read or be with friends in the intervening space, there would be an exhibition space at the back, and every office simply has to have a daybed and a piano. In order not to seem lazy, I call the daybed a "casting couch". My well-versed choice of sexist labels affords the best protection! The piano would be used every Sunday for my vocal training lessons with Janko Zannos. We came across the professor of vocal training through the Vienna Boys Choir, and he is a member of our innermost circle of like-minded people. Leisurely and without effort, we would give voice to our bar classics for ourselves and for anyone wandering by the comptoir at that moment. The passageway to the back was ideal for a swing. In the bright front section, I would hold meetings, but would sit most of the time at my desk writing and pursuing my various occupations. And all around me, on the very high walls that had first to be painted green, would hang art. I would design the shop window displays to be tempting and mad all at once, and the door would always be open. A few interim steps needed to be taken. The conversion work during the pandemic was a challenge. Along the way, the architect warned me that I was heading for unhappiness in the hole. Painted green? Open onto the street? No practical floor tiles, as beige as the anoraks of golfing grannies? I wasn't about to be talked out of my love. I largely remained stalwart and happy to take the decisions. This way, that way, and this way

Evolution of Schmerlingplatz → 216

again – they’d all be amazed. My husband backed me up, told me not to give ground, although there were plenty of obstacles. As the details for the comptoir developed, it soon emerged that Klaus was happy to be an occasional guest, drop by for a coffee, a chat. However, he had just put a lot of energy into the museum. Just as in collections where a foundation is set up and does a dummy run during the collector’s lifetime, my husband had already passed on the baton. He wanted to enjoy things, sit back and be amazed, and listen to things. But he did not want to be in the limelight. No longer. If I found the going too rough in the limelight while implementing my plans, then a friend was at hand to enter the fray. Jürgen Sturany turned the conversion into a project and devised a few charts and lists so that it all looked more like Ken and less like Barbie. And things swiftly started progressing again. I was in need of the support and was happy to accept it. Another novelty: I don’t have to do everything myself. In the final instance, everyone weighed in, even those who thought I was quite insane. Some people simply did their job, others were so busy in their heads with the pandemic and other things that they simply did the very next thing that needed doing without asking that closely; sometimes I did have the feeling that tradesmen thought it was all so ridiculous, she must have a hidden plan. So. Let’s wait and see whether she comes a cropper or something comes of it all. Today, the one or other tradesman still drops by and readily concedes that they might not have been able to imagine it, but in fact it really is marvelous.

I'm singing agai[n]

Coffee always smells better than it tastes. In this regard, too, the comptoir defies the everyday ordinary. Head-over-heels, I immediately had the idea of what it would be like once Internet, windows, door, power, heating, and water were installed (here in order of priority. Reality was then even better, much better. The comptoir is like an embrace. Warm and familiar and strengthening. The space is like an ever-present tailwind. The promise was there right from the beginning: I'd be able to do everything here. I survived the conversion period thanks to this quiet, enjoyable sense of certainty. During the construction work, I repeatedly found myself at the door, looking into my future work venue, a bizarre proscenium stage! I was usually not able to step inside because in the few weeks that the process was to last (again something quite out of the ordinary) very many tradesmen were all at work at once, like in one of the games where you have to find the hidden objects. I considered it of great benefit that the construction work was being professionally managed, and I could watch it all from the outside. It was good to have the time to train my own eye and imagine how the premises would look to others. Every pending embrace made me vulnerable. That was part and parcel of things. I therefore opened my heart and welcomed the good promise. Just like buying a piece of art and then ascertaining, when integrating it into the household, into the collection, and into the storeroom, that the size and effect (specifically its simultaneous effect with the items already there) holds many a surprise in store, first embraces are always unlike what you imagined. Is it like that for everyone? As a court-appointed expert, I am specialized in the field of sculpture and very good at anticipating things. Albeit evidently only part-aspects. Meaning I can judge whether a format fits. What it feels like cannot be sensed in advance. Which brings me back to the special, expansive sculptures of Angela Glajcar. After all the years and as editor of her catalogue raisonné, I am very familiar with her work, but clearly only she can sense in advance the spatial experiences that she then creates. I believe spatial experiences are something that cannot be anticipated. I looked forward to the space, imagining it as in a photo rather than as a feeling, and the pleasant, beautiful overlap of expectation and emerging reality was perfectly glorious to enjoy. The comptoir was more spacious than expected, offered more different spaces to tarry a while, to talk, to contemplate than I had anticipated, and the spatial atmosphere that arose was for me like Africa: honest, genuine, clear.

I received warnings from all sides that I should not place myself in the limelight in such a way. Would I be able to concentrate, wouldn't people keep dropping in, here, in the heart of town, and not least: Was it not perhaps even dangerous? I did not share these reservations. On the contrary. I had loved my time as a gallery assistant in Amsterdam specifically because of the open houses and apartments bereft of curtains. Without being able to exactly say why I had a view on this, something along the lines of: "What is there to see, anyway? This is how people live. They eat, play, talk with the kids, drink, laugh, argue. Why should that be hidden away?" I therefore insisted that the Dutch streak in me was "totally in favor", and I could do things that way and could, if necessary, withdraw; no, actually this was my real nature. That is definitely not the case. I have no ancestors in this regard, let alone role models or experiences of my own. To be honest, the opposite is true. Although I grew up in solitude, factually without neighbors and, as the real estate agents would say, with a view out that no one could obstruct, my mother nevertheless set great store by seclusion from the outside world. We in fact had a fierce dispute over a curtain she insisted on hanging in a window. She considered me a terrorist, as I had torn down said textile item. The improbable case of a chance passer-by out walking being able, if he could lean sufficiently far over the garden gate, to glimpse me at my desk was reason enough for her to block out the free view that extended as far as the forest emerging vaguely blue on the horizon. One of my cousins said in such situations that the midwife had brought me along in her bag. Somehow, I did not fit in. A great, mad, subversive symbol by way of fantastic explanation as to why I did not even feel the need to set myself off from the world or have done things differently out of defiance. For me, many things are completely normal, not special, not rebellious, not elitist, but simply "normal". Despite the shop window through which I can be seen and despite the forever open door, to my mind the comptoir offers me and my thoughts a great deal of protection. Only very rarely do strange people come in, and only once was I unable to handle the situation, when, suddenly, a Newfoundland dog stood next to my desk and in dozy-dog manner gazed at me with big open eyes. After a while, his charming owner managed to retrieve him, but the big dog was still busy blinking at me. The scene was like a film still, until a third party set life in motion again. I talked to the dog, trying to convince it to leave and that there was nothing he would like in the comptoir, and he simply blinked with his big eyes. The basic mood in the comptoir is joyful. Passers-by take photos of the window displays, some pop in and look at the space and with it the art, without engaging in conversation with me. People thank me and go on their way, some stay for a chat, many people drop by repeatedly. In the course of a day, people greet me through the window, often with a wave. Essentially, all daily life in the comptoir obeys the wisdom that the shortest link between two people is a smile. Conversations ensue. Long gone are the days of boastful, self-indulgent facts about art. Conversations about art now have a completely different quality. People engage more warmly with art. Of course, this also has to do with me, that I can really enthuse and be more infectious in the mood that now prevails. I've put down my roots in the comptoir, and the neighborhood lives with the space. Sometimes, my husband stands outside the window just like the passers-by who don't know me and holds his sides from laughing. If I'm out and about in the neighborhood, children greet me on the street. Their parents ask how they know me. Children are simply better at playing "Memory", they recognize me in a different setting.

Things unpleasant occur, somehow invariably, only through events in the old established formats. In other words, initially old mistakes were repeated, but the space can't perform everything. I expected too much of it. A large part evidently stems from me alone. The fact that this format for presenting the collection has something delightfully light about it most probably stems, or so closer inspection suggests, from my having something to do in the comptoir. As a result, I now sit less in the limelight and in the glasshouse than I previously did in the fortress-like museum building. Because I work and communicate casually with passers-by and guests, and, first and foremost, do not expect anything in particular. Most of the time, I am busy compiling my expert opinions, writing other texts, or discharging administrative duties. I hold lectures or take part in training sessions. Previously, the work had to be done if guests arrived because of the art. On the back of recognizing that first a casual mood and second a one-on-one or small group are the best formats for me, I avoid the ordeal of large groups from associations of friends and the like. Then there are the parties in the comptoir that are slowly but surely becoming the talk of the town. Once again following in the footsteps of the legendary Peggy Guggenheim, and very welcome she would be.

Shop window
Schmerlingplatz → 219

Performative reception

The form found is, in the final analysis, just like the art I appreciate most, namely performative. No standing around at a loss any longer, which would predominate in the setting, and no one exhausted by full-on frontal lectures. Rather, my answers to guests' questions feel a bit like exclusive city guided tours, also coupled with a shot of stand-up comedy. If someone responds strongly, for example to the works by Matthias Herrmann, I think of my actor colleague with the gynecologist father and say: "I have hung it up because I like it." Like with any good joke, I also don't forget to add, with as neutral a look on my face as possible, that "Hey, it's a girls' office."

The duly becoming approach to art. The tamed approach to art (see LOOK AT ME! CHECKPOINTS OF AN ART COLLECTION [Spector Books, 2018], p. 105). That's now all a matter of the past. Today, precious items may even get hung in the bathroom. If I'm asked why, it's back to comedy. Where else does one have enough peace and quiet to consider them? Following up with: It's also cruel, because while otherwise you can always start chattering, in the bathroom you're initially alone with your helplessness or your urge to chat and can't immediately start talking about the piece. In order to keep the regularity of the cascade of jokes going, I then add: Not that this is good for the men among us, as we all know that they can't do two things at once. Such enjoyable dialogs never cease to energize me. Things never stop at the joke, but the laughter or amazement always acts as the stumbling stone into something else. And if not, well, hey, at least one had a healthy laugh together. For me, symposia and cultivated-distanced talks are not a filling meal in themselves. I like to be effusive, best of all intoxicated by art and the poetry of things. Many of the artistic posi-

Matthias Herrmann
8×10'#/48 (PAINTING), TEXT: ED HARRIS → 218

tions in the collection focus accordingly on the poetry of things, Andrei Roiter – Thomas Demand – Louise Lawler – Cindy Sherman. The curios seem to have wandered from the images into the comptoir's shop window. As a young woman, I read an article about someone visiting Cindy Sherman's studio. It described how bizarre her inventory of materials was. Parts of dolls, costumes, eyes, legs, arms. The shop window takes up this depository of ideas. Like no other place I have inhabited before, the provocatively vulgar that lacks any distance, the aphorisms, and the amusing, sweet, associatively arranged curios truly represent my innermost being. I sometimes find other people's ebullience and their associations frightening. One good example of this is Jonathan Meese, whose monstrous associations I find just that. I can't decipher him, and I don't need to. I see my personal maturation process has gifted me the certainty that I no longer have to see with a knowing eye, as if I could decipher everything and discern every allusion as though writing a term paper. Even if I could. And this learning curve has also taught me to empathize with other persons' irritation. What instills me with more fear than others' effusiveness is their lack of anything to say. The years in the comptoir, starting with the shop window and continuing with the many invitations to step inside and view the interior are to me like an easy-access offer to be with me, but not neutrally. My work provides the protection. So I am now like the Lilliputians in the theme park; people can watch me at work, wave. What happens if someone steps in the door is an open question, but it is the friendliness of strangers and not any sense of bitter prejudice that wafts through the door. I experience many nice things. Guests who have announced themselves in advance alternate with art people who were "next door" in the museum quarter and spot the art through the window, or passers-by who walk past every day and at some point dare to stop for a chat. Alongside the loans business for the collection with very important museums, I also loan out items from the shop window. Max from the neighborhood (three years old) sometimes takes the helicopter home with him, other times the sweeper. Sometimes he simply stays and plays with the things that belong to my sons, which they can't find a use for at that precise moment. He immerses himself completely in what he is doing. I take part or watch him and try and learn something. I find it difficult to immerse myself in something and to be aimless. However, perhaps the way Max interacts with things only looks aimless to me. Perhaps Max takes his game as seriously as Kurt who, sitting on the beach in the sand and asked what he was concerning himself with, replied most seriously: "I'm just doing my work." What I seek to realize in the comptoir is a game that does not need to be primarily useful and comprehensible. I don't want to play the whelp and toy around with something, and the adults are happy because that way I learn to hunt. My game is meant to be as free of purpose as art. Just as sex only very rarely serves reproduction. When Elisabeth von Samsonow anointed me Pretzel Goddess, in one sense it seemed completely natural to me. At any rate, to me my thoughts seem sufficiently twisted and the shifting back and forth between sublimeness, a strong education, and rebellious silliness goes a long way in my case. There was a time when I penned so-called travelogs, and a strange blog it was. Less of a report in the narrow sense of the term. What I experienced I proceeded to transform into fantastic cabaret-like glosses. In my comptoir, I have the opportunity to visualize these skeins of thoughts. Together with Max, I renew and expand my skills as regards installations. I find a path to important linkages by assembling things that are often very loosely associated with art. Instagram has taken the potential to interlock and visualize meaning to completely new levels.

There was a time when making models of things seemed strange to me. I even tried to avoid having to imitate things back in my school days. The content of the theoretical art lessons was tough, which played into my hands. By contrast, the practical part I found hard going. How to achieve something with my limited skills? Thanks to the comptoir with its range of expressive opportunities, the emphasis is on approaching the virtuosity of artists with a touch of charm and zest, doffing my cap to them rather than exploiting someone else's ideas. In this way, a sculpture by Reinhard Mucha, in which three small stools lean against one another, turns into three loaves of bread, which in turn morph into three smartphones. An early piece by Tony Cragg, consisting of a ladder, casting molds, and hooks, is translated into toast, cheese, and potatoes, and promptly eaten. The architecture of the works is transformed into any manner of things, with due reference to the scale and the materials in order to approximate the fragile balance innate to them and to get a sense of my own feel for these works. Something like this would have been inconceivable before the comptoir came into my life. For me, school was followed by studying law. As a result, all forms of imitation and potentially epigonal behavior became ever more suspect. Essentially, I acted as if I were suing myself for abuse of copyright. When I first came into contact with the collection that is today part of my life, a lamp that, formally speaking, resembled a section in a Konrad Klapheck image, had been placed on the floor in front of the painting; simply there, as if the two objects belonged together. Now that I found embarrassing.

Reinhard Mucha
ALTBAU GEGEN NEUBAU (OLD BUILD VS. NEW BUILD) → 217

Rave community

Alongside the well-behaved events with the collection, this state of being embarrassed by how I empowered myself in engaging with art was my well-mannered baseline. And was limiting. Bidding farewell to the white-cube aesthetics and the related tame approach to art was the key for me to forge my own bond to the collection. Because, as said, collecting has to have a function in your own biography. In the life of the generation of post-war entrepreneurs in Germany, trials of courage, pre-empting daring business ventures, and pseudo-feudal self-positioning were among the motivations. And now I had found my own motivation: the yearning for a happy childhood. Suitable settings to live a happy childhood were at hand. Instead of cops and robbers, instead of pirates, I adapted the aestheticization of danger from the portraits by Rosemarie Trockel. There, the focus is on COVID, and the way I hold my hand looks like smoking. Thus, the Barbies in the dolls' house push shopping carts filled to the brim with cigars and sharp cigarettes along beneath the cannabis plant. And wear dirndls and gothic attire. The Barbies look just like me. And the level of how I treat my appearance, my reality as a blonde fashion lover and model, can always be sensed here. Just as the collection is teaming with dwarves, gnomes, and wights, now strange creatures are also on the move in the shop window.

Doll: Susanne Bisovsky → 218

I made a mouse from a washcloth, called it the Prince of Dubai and included the prince in the colorful collection of curios in the shop window. The name is borrowed from a real criminal lawsuit. A marriage impostor in Berlin called himself the Prince of Dubai. The energy the criminal had had in playing the part of a real person who served the women's wish for a fairytale was reduced here to a pocket-sized facecloth figure, and that I liked.

Con artist Anna Sorokin assembled a persona for herself from bits taken from various celebrities. With a little effort, people could have exposed her. The Prince of Dubai, by contrast, acted the part of someone who actually existed. What chutzpah! And what does it say about the people who wanted to believe they had links with the real Prince of Dubai? I was subsequently accused rigorously of appropriating the name from a foreign culture and trivializing romance scamming. Forging art is likewise no peccadillo, but also a kind of tricking someone's love. In the fake images, skillfully forged in line with our expectations from the core of an artist's oeuvre, one can sense the mean exploitation of our emotions. If forged images hang on museum walls, then the museum's task of preserving, researching, and educating is inverted into presenting an inauthentic artistic expression. Usually, I am happy if I see things that way. If a discussion then ensues about it, all the better, and I gladly take part. However, the shop window
1 is just like collections when they are bestowed on someone or something, no (hi)stories are provided along with them, and the heirs are tantamount to archaeologists who only see the artifacts, but not their meaning. Some things remain cryptic, and that is always tolerable. I find it a great benefit to (increasingly) enjoy the one or other ambiguity of different interpretations. For the imbalance between what is said and what remains unsaid fundamentally foxes me. On the one hand, in my opinion things are constantly talked to death. At the same time, things that I believe definitely need to be clarified never get discussed. I do not in any way like the feeling of impotence I then have. At long last, I have found a way of solving this. Communicating through joyful intimation, simply letting things stand as they are. Without commentary. Not solved. Is that not what art is about? Where discourse ends…

Creating the Prince of Dubai → 218

I know that life doesn’t ge serious

In the shop window, I display casual daily slogans to encourage offbeat ideas: “I know that life doesn’t get serious.” Or: “Whoever claims that consumerism doesn’t make you happy shops in the wrong store.” Don’t bash consumerism. Seen in this light, my approach to art has something to do with my profession after all. Because in my daily dealings with artists and collectors, I am forever being confronted with the extreme emotions of my clients. Artists fear no longer making good art because they become happy individuals; collectors indulge in fantasies of omnipotence and heirs in their greed. In the past, I often felt myself dry and lackluster compared to my clients. Because my clients were forever reporting on their massive emotions. In the course of time, I realized that they set great store by having truly massive, oh-so-significant, huge feelings. It was quite irrelevant whether the feelings were positive or negative. What counted was the intensity. Family bonds relied on these dramatically monstrous feelings. Compared to this, I was somehow out of place and even found myself being told that what I had considered to be a sense of balance was actually my lack of passion. In my dealings with the collection, I thus also explore the challenges of my profession and air the big emotions that blow in my face. The apodictic side to my profession of lawyer and court-appointed expert is parodied and neutralized by stardust and daydreams. The insistence that there are two parties to the litigation, and that at the end of the day one will win, always seemed to me a bit like kindergarten. There had to be much more than that. I find a starting point in the work of artists who, to my mind, have preserved or reconquered magic in the use of language. Andrei Roiter grew up with Cyrillic letters, and assigning sounds to our language and thus to our written script has

Tony Cragg, Andrei Roiter, Christian Frosch, Sasa, Photo: Koko Usami → 219

remained pleasantly foreign to him. The use of a language spoken in a foreign tongue, in this case English, is also magical. Jonathan Meese speaks and sings in one long daydreamy associative sequence. Even the initiate can hardly work out the transferences and references. All that is clear is that there are deeper ties, and the thoughts aren't meant to stand up to strong intellectual scrutiny anyway. Ferdinand Kriwet creates poetry with his works. I love walking among the works of lyrical positions. The joy in thinking and even more in dreaming, the joy in addressing themes, is something that should spark and sparkle and no longer be repelled. My somewhat musty child-like being has also found a solution to turning magic into verbalized thought. Externally, the decision was blessed by the prosaic explanation that I would do better in the elite school if I always used the language of instruction. The truth, however, is that the decision on entering boarding school to speak the language as it was written rather than the dialect of my family
3 at home gave handling isolation a clear shape. Speaking was suddenly like singing a French chanson, the contents of which you do not understand for a minute and which only talks to you in intimations.

Use your Imagination (Billy Bragg

I grew up with the slogans of the student uprisings ringing in my ears. “Imagine there’s a war and no one goes.” Or: “We’ll save the world, I say, and people laugh at me, but if everyone thought that way then we would long since have done it.” In my engagement with art, I have come to strongly respect the collector’s resolute commitment. “Simply do it.” That’s what my husband told himself after arriving at the beginning of his remarkable professional career. As a minor tax officer together with his colleague Franz-Josef (who decades later was to arrange for us to meet), during the morning break and over sandwiches and thermos-flask coffee he announced the revolution. Crazy. And yet it 2
turned into a large corporation. Meaning it wasn’t that silly. Today, I can find pleasure in such megalomania. I have only come to appreciate the intensity and emphasis, the creative energy and zest of artists by immersing myself in art that is simply there. Seen from the outside, for me, for all my decades of being active in the art market, this was something I could not see.

I am evidently not a strong enough hedonist to immoderately collect. That is a very ambivalent insight into my own being. It is no doubt less strenuous my way. Life is more contemplative. To say “I don’t need that” is, however, also to remain in your comfort zone, and the indeterminate wish to experience the intoxication of excess remains. The playful engagement with the collection’s holdings which, like all duties in this world, can crush you with their facticity, now proves to be a driving force, a source of great energy for a pleasurable approach to the challenges of life and the specific task of assuming responsibility. If the children of collectors are told in the context of inheriting that they should continue, then they are actually being told that they should play the same game as their ancestors. Meaning someone else's game. Then they will experience a situation offering little scope. No one wants to be a spoilsport, but who wants to act according to outside and often opaque game rules? An art collection is not a board game which, if you are unlucky, sees you not passing Go or getting chucked out just before you reach the finishing line. The great gain from engaging with the collection was the discovery that I could invent my own game. It became so good the moment I felt the individual possibilities rather than the restrictions. The insight that anyone assuming responsibility for a collection or another comparable task needs to be strong and adult, meaning rational, was "only right to a certain extent". Thankfully I have succeeded in hearing the tempting promise the collection whispered to me: "Play with me!"

Evolution of Schmerlingplatz
Photos: Jürgen T. Sturany

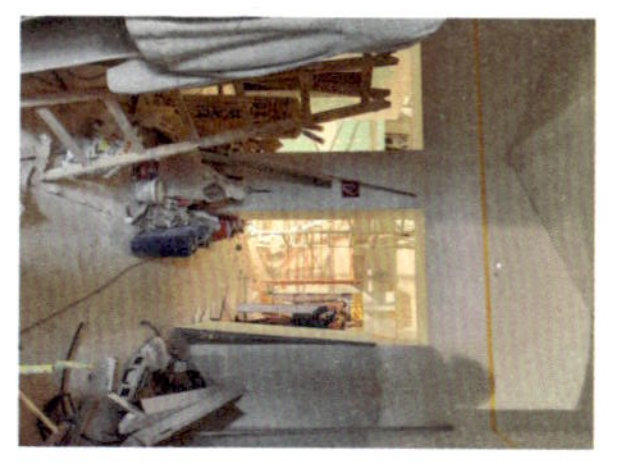

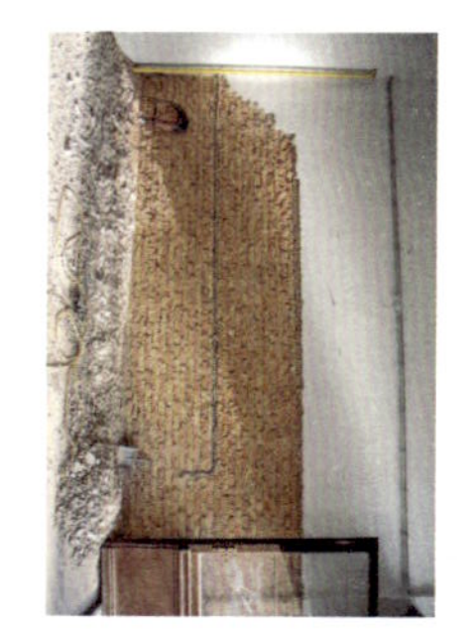

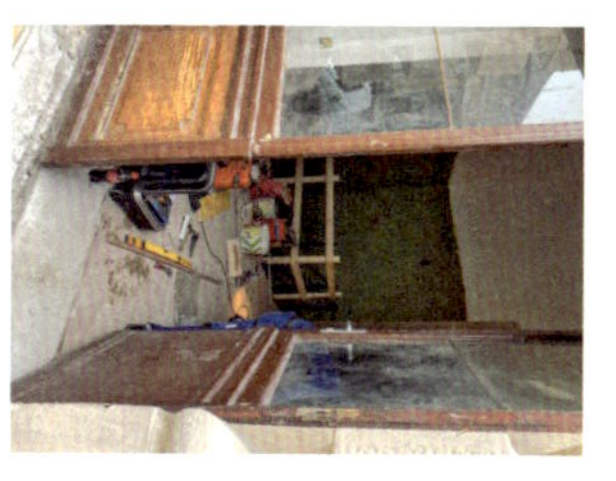

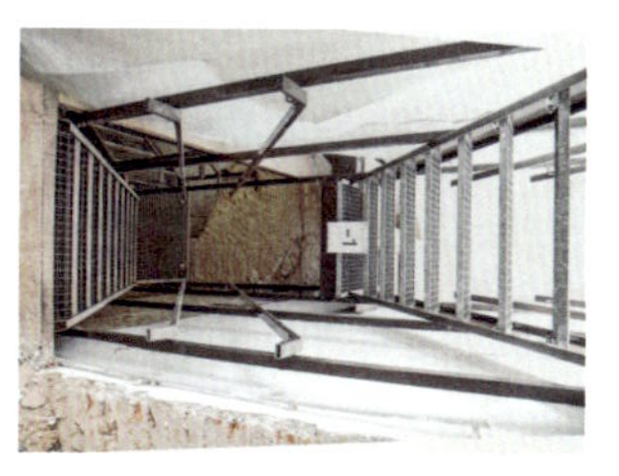

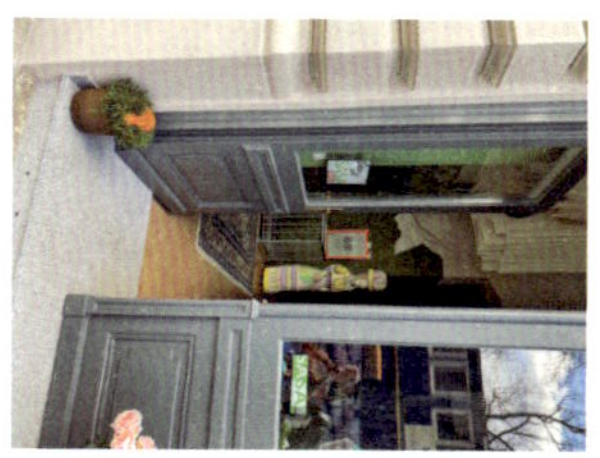

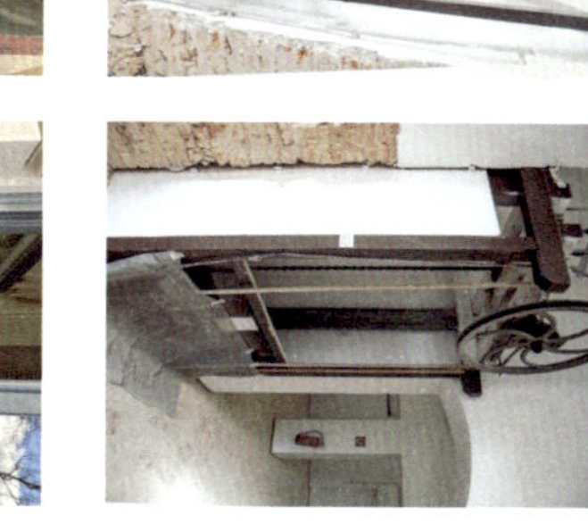

Angela Glajcar
DREAMCATCHER – TRAUMFÄNGER

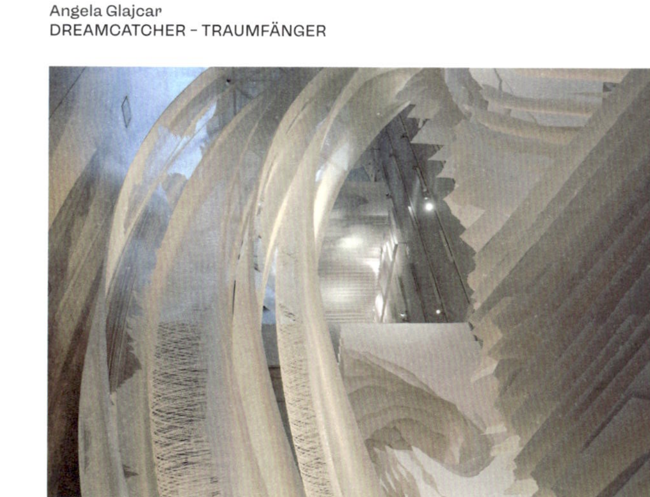

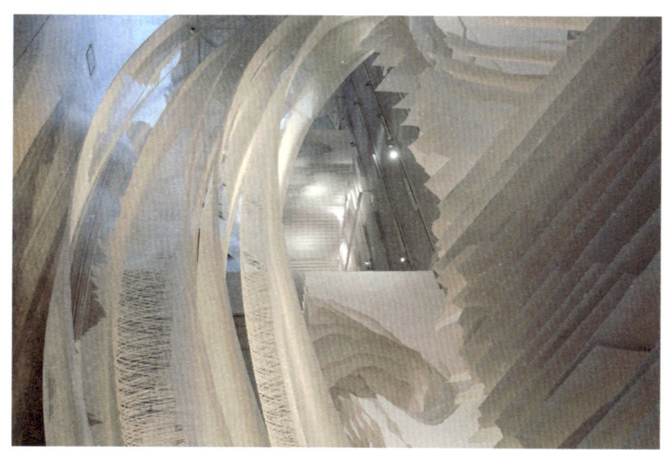

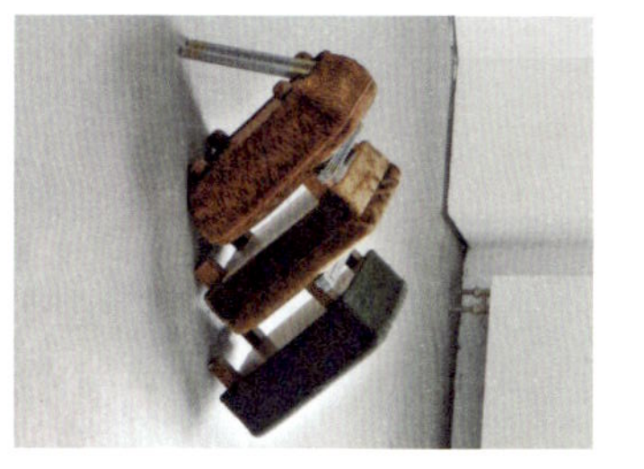

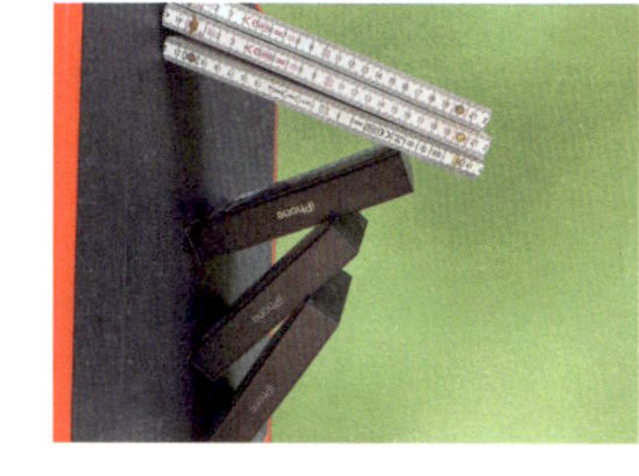

Reinhard Mucha
ALTBAU GEGEN NEUBAU, (OLD BUILD VS. NEW BUILD) Adaptations

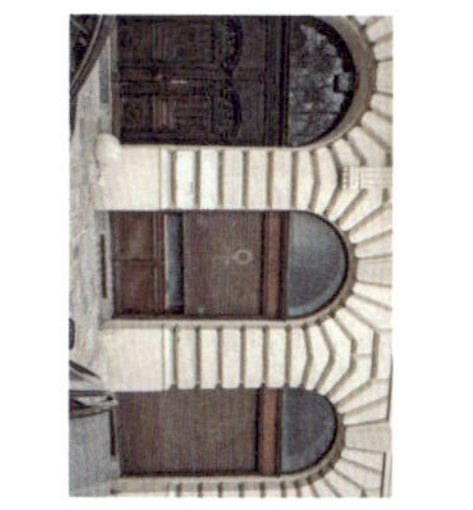

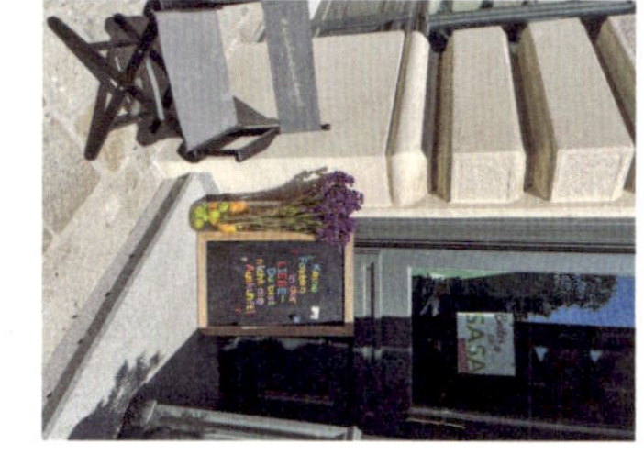

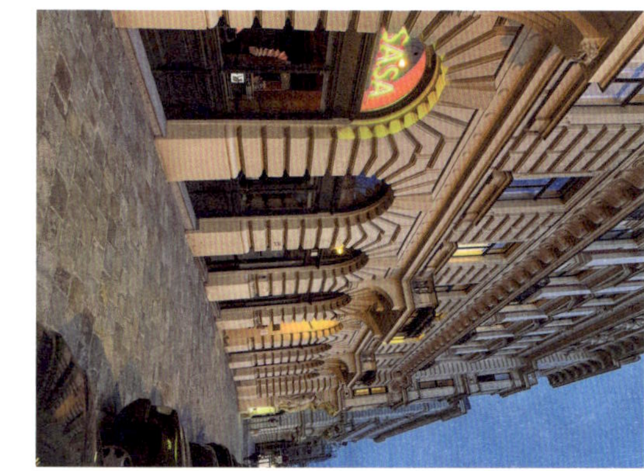

Schmerlingplatz

Matthias Herrmann,
Adaptations

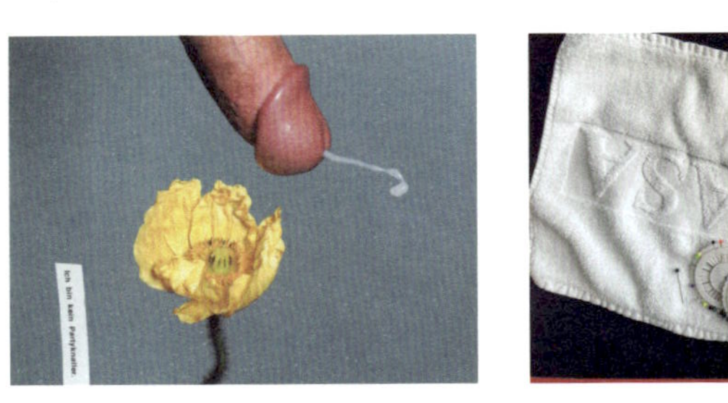

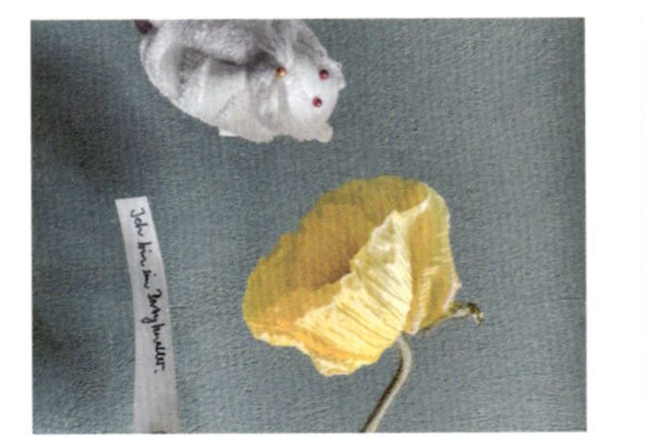

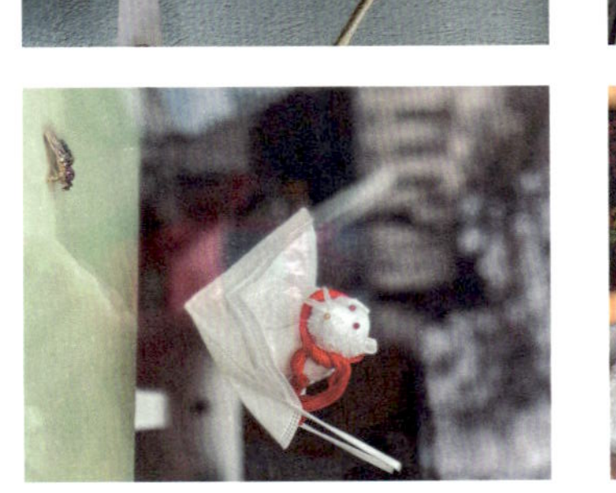

Creating the Prince of Dubai
Prince of Dubai by Alexandra Bircken and
on the r. doll by Susanne Bisovsky

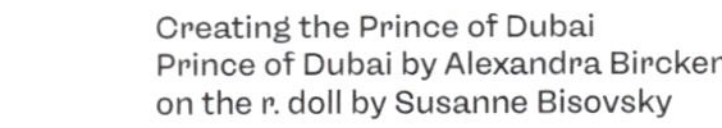

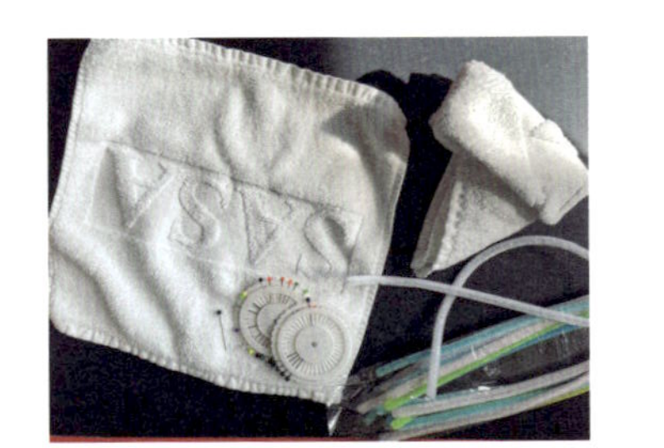

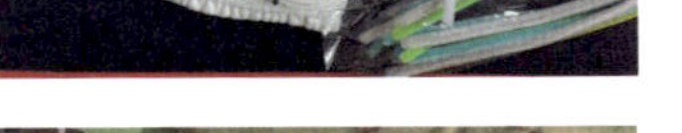

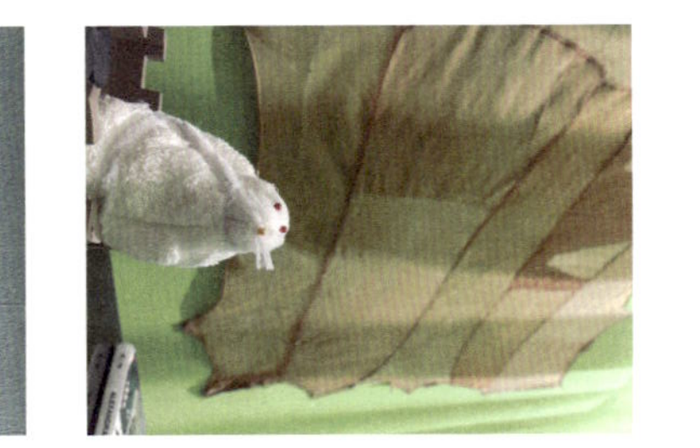

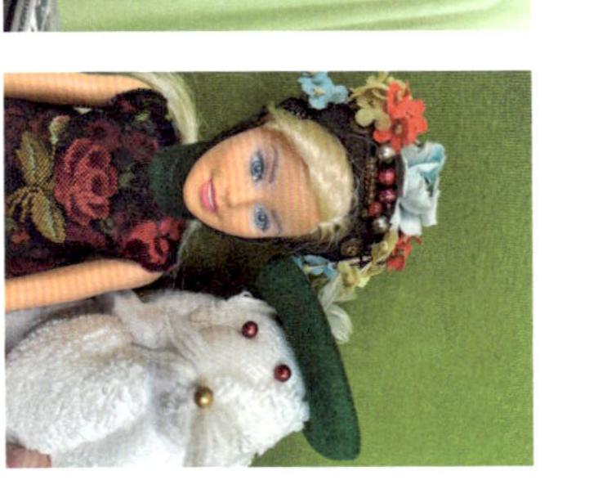

Doll: Susanne Bisovsky,
Adaptation for the shop window

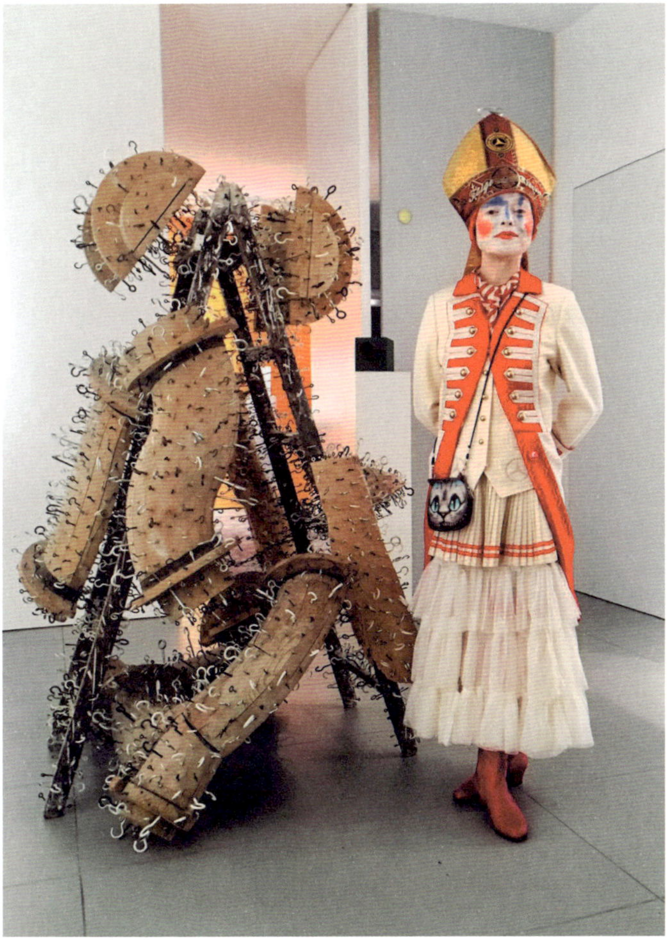

Tony Cragg, Andrei Roiter, Christian Frosch, Sasa,
Photo: Koko Usami

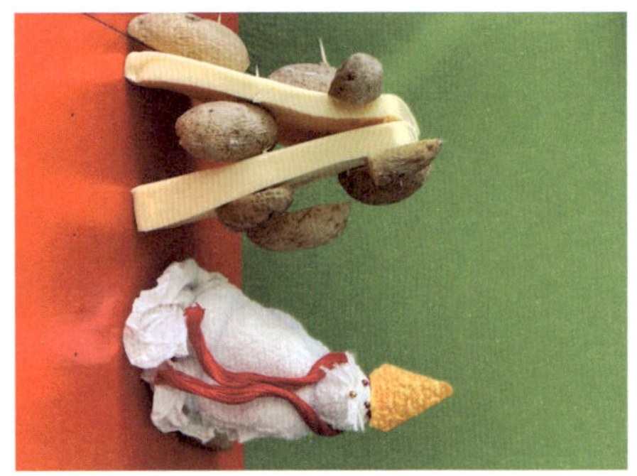

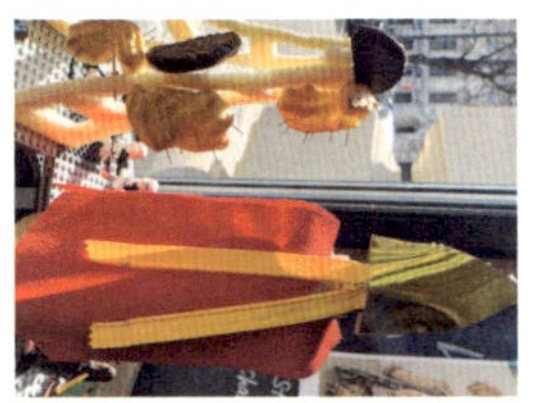

Tony Cragg
Adaptations

“Don’t fuck with writers

After “Look at me! Checkpoints of an Art Collection” I was relieved to have unraveled the tricky task of creating a collection and of having mastered the actual transition. Now, after a few years living with the art, I am at peace with things and enjoy life. Many thanks to all of you who have helped with the thinking, the work, and have laughed along with me in this period of re-invention. Everyone who feels I might mean them: You are meant. And some of you in more roles than one: soul brothers and sisters, artists, in particular Angela Glajcar and Elisabeth von Samsonow, my nuclear family (first and foremost: Klaus), the kids (Jakob and Konrad of course, and all the other children who have semi-adopted us, not to mention next-door’s child Max), gallerists, ancestors, clients, passers-by, public patio pals… don’t feel you’ve been cannibalized, but appreciate in the descriptions of your good selves how marvelously inspiring you all are. Special thanks go directly to those involved in producing the book. My thanks go to the photographers. My special thanks go to Vlad Dobre for the pleasurable cover shoot and to my soulmate Markus Spatzier, who curated the cover and handled the costume design for it. Many thanks to models Gerhard, Godfrey, Godwin, Kiril, Luca, Samuel, and all the others who placed their bodies (and not just their souls and great thoughts) in the service of this book. I deeply admire Michael Gais for having once

we will describe you.”

again taken a psychotically exaggerated briefing and turned it into the design for a beautiful book. Many thanks to Christian Wöllecke for his sensitive editing. Many thanks to Jeremy Gaines who shouldered the task of turning this intricate book into English and pleasantly surprised me. My publisher Spector Books was always supportively at my side for the long journey from the beginning of “Look at me” through to publication of “Play with me”. The calm presence of Jan Wenzel, with all his intelligent questions and tempting confidence, was indispensable throughout.
I would like to sincerely thank everyone involved in the COMPTOIR project. In particular Patrick Arzberger (That’ll be a smash!), Paul Fruhmann (I want you!), Mario Fuchs (Yes. No. That’s nonsense.), Slavisa Tatic (Really? Seriously?), Josef Oswald (We can fix it!), Bernd Rossbacher (Be with you in a second!), Jürgen T. Sturany (I’ve prepared the Excel charts!), Günther Pfleger (That’s art? Aha.), and all the others, too.

To a playful future!

Sasa Hanten-Schmidt, Vienna, 2023

Making-of Cover

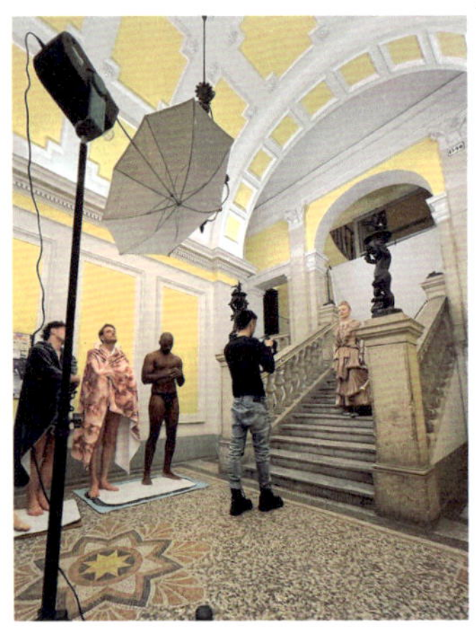

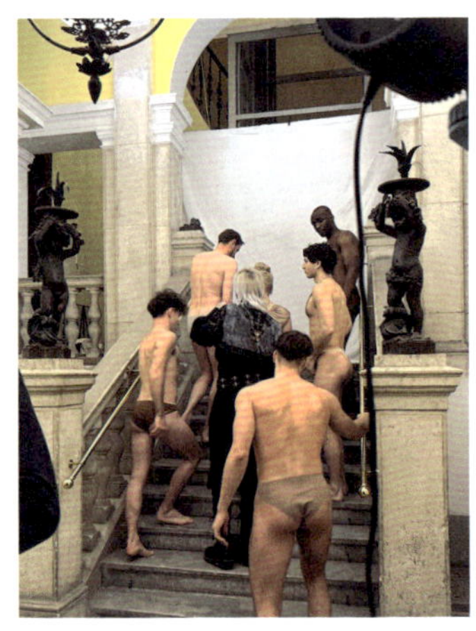

2

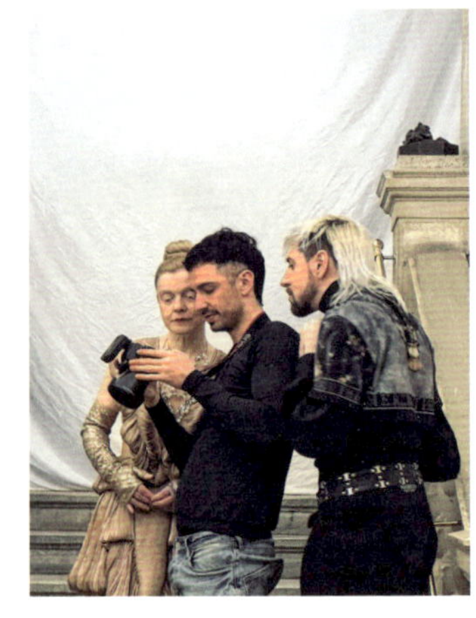

Sasa, Vlad Dobre, Markus Spatzier
Photo: Angela Glajcar

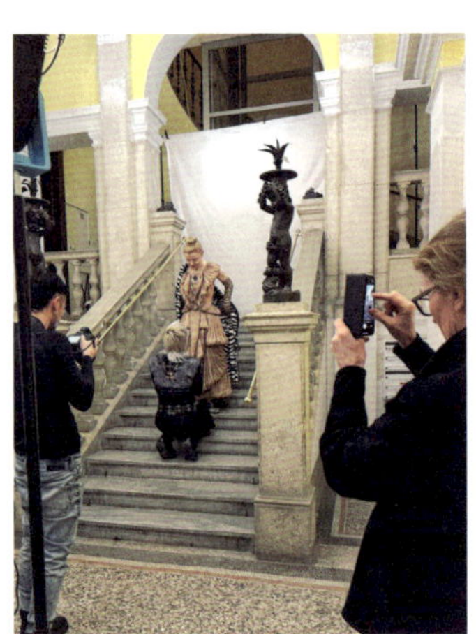

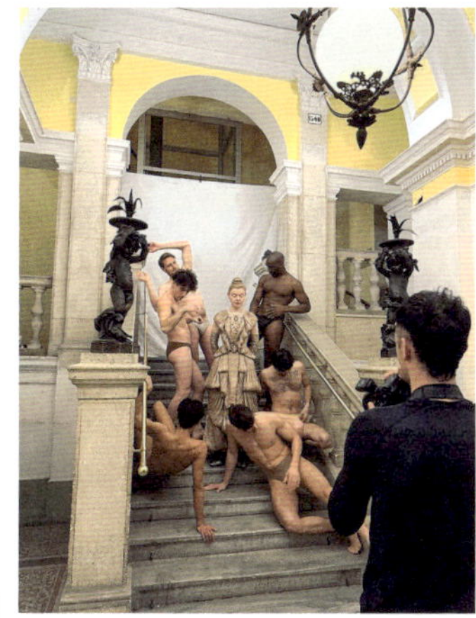

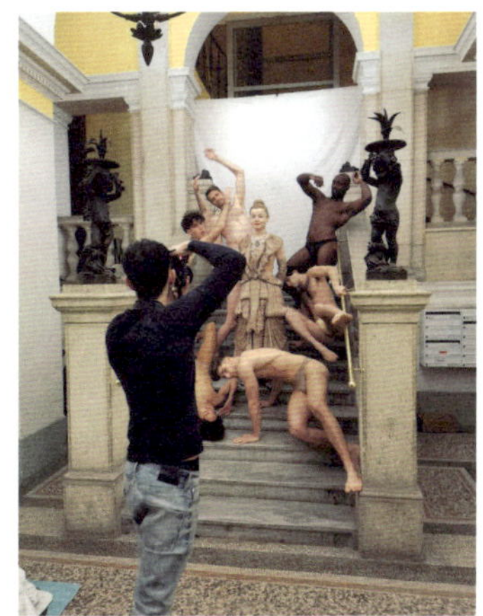

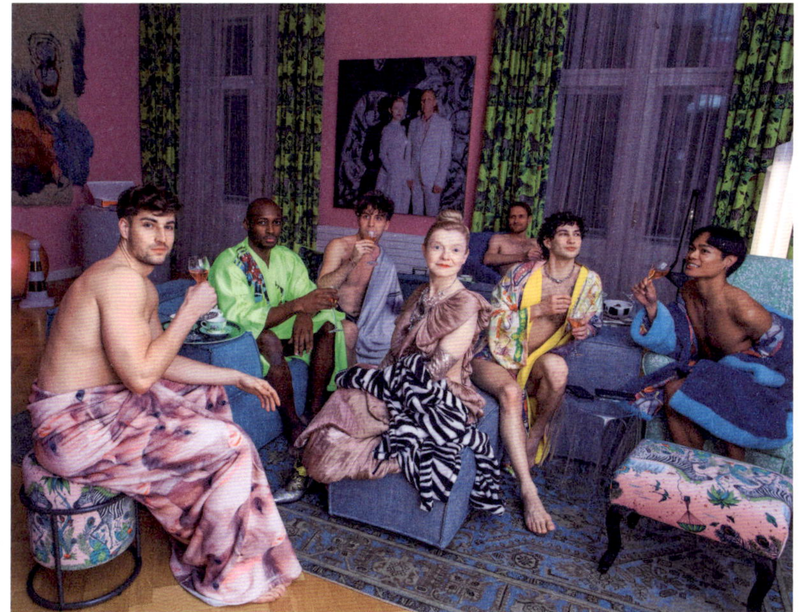

Samuel, Godfrey, Kiril, Sasa, Gerhard, Luca, Godwin

Imprint

Text: Sasa Hanten-Schmidt
English translation: Jeremy Gaines,
Proofreading: Katy Fowler, Dirk Beyer,
Mary Anne Cassel Meyer
Copy editor: Christian Wöllecke
PR: Franciska JC Schmitt
Design: QWER, Michael Gais
Image processing: PPP, Cologne
Printed by: Gutenberg Beuys
Feindruckerei GmbH

Published by:
Spector Books
Harkortstraße 10
04107 Leipzig
www.spectorbooks.com

Distribution:
Germany, Austria: GVA, Gemeinsame
Verlagsauslieferung Göttingen
GmbH&Co. KG, www.gva-verlage.de
Switzerland: AVA Verlagsauslieferung AG,
www.ava.ch
France, Belgium: Interart Paris,
www.interart.fr
UK: Central Books Ltd,
www.centralbooks.com
USA, Canada, Central and South
America, Africa: ARTBOOK/ D.A.P.,
www.artbook.com
South Korea: The Book Society,
www.thebooksociety.org
Japan: twelvebooks,
www.twelve-books.com
Australia, New Zealand: Perimeter
Distribution,
www.perimeterdistribution.com

Photos: Maximilian Anelli-Monti
(Clegg & Guttmann), Maximilian
Brucker (Elisabeth von Samsonow), Vlad
Dobre (Cover, Making-of), Sasa Fuis
(Museum Cologne), Bettina Fürst-Fastré,
Angela Glajcar, Sasa Hanten-Schmidt,
Werner Lieberknecht (Flat Vienna),
Jürgen T. Sturany, Koko Usami (Sasa
and Tony Cragg)
Cover idea: Markus Spatzier, Manufaktur
Herzblut Vienna
Models: Gerhard, Godfrey, Godwin,
Kiril, Luca, Samuel

Many thanks to Stella Models, Galerie
Loock Berlin (Gabriele Stötzer) and
the Hanten-Schmidt-Foundation.

1st edition
Printed in Germany
ISBN 978-3-95905-685-4

A driving force behind:

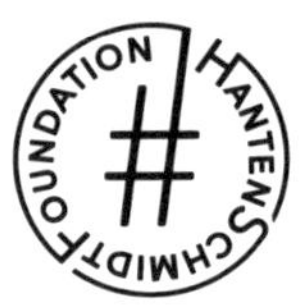